Natural Disasters as a Catalyst for Social Capital

A Study of the 500-Year Flood in Cedar Rapids, Iowa

Kevin F. Adler

University Press of America,® Inc.

Lanham • Boulder • New York • Toronto • Plymouth, UK

Copyright © 2015 by University Press of America,® Inc.
4501 Forbes Boulevard, Suite 200, Lanham, Maryland 20706
UPA Acquisitions Department (301) 459-3366

Unit A, Whitacre Mews, 26-34 Stannary Street,
London SE11 4AB, United Kingdom

Printed in the United States of America
British Library Cataloguing in Publication Information Available

Library of Congress Control Number: 2014947716
ISBN: 978-0-7618-6466-0 (paper : alk. paper)—ISBN: 978-0-7618-6467-7 (electronic)

Cover photo republished with permission © 2014 Iowa SourceMedia Group, Cedar Rapids, Iowa.

Excerpts from the following chapter have been reprinted throughout *Natural Disasters as a Catalyst for Social Capital*: Copyright © 2010 From "Social Capital after a Disaster: A Case Study of the 2008 Flood in Cedar Rapids, Iowa" in *Community Disaster Recovery and Resiliency: Exploring Global Opportunities and Challenges*, edited by DeMond S. Miller and Jason David Rivera, chapter authored by Kevin F. Adler. Reproduced by permission of Taylor and Francis Group, LLC, a division of Informa plc.

Maps in Appendix 2 courtesy of the City of Cedar Rapids GIS Department.

∞™ The paper used in this publication meets the minimum requirements of American National Standard for Information Sciences Permanence of Paper for Printed Library Materials, ANSI/NISO Z39.48-1992.

Contents

Preface

I grew up in a small town with a small family. From a young age, I was taught to look at neighbors, friends, and classmates as an extension of my family. I trusted others to help me meet my needs, be they emotional (companionship, mutual support, cooperation), security (bicycling around town, emergency response), or professional (finding jobs, receiving mentorship). My worldview was largely framed by social capital before I had heard of the term.

I first came across the concept of social capital while I was in college. At the same time I discovered social capital's importance as an indicator of civic health, I learned about its apparent decline in the United States since the late 1960s, as measured by social trust, civic engagement, sense of togetherness, and the like.

I took this loss personally. I was alarmed at the thought that the very social fabric of the United States in which I was so tightly wound was unravelling. I wanted to understand why this was happening, and put a stop to it.

In his seminal book *Bowling Alone*, Robert Putnam postulates that the fuzzy notion of "generational change" is the primary culprit for social capital's marked decline in the United States. Something about the shared sacrifices and common enemy of World War II brought a generation together, whereas a polarizing war in Vietnam and the social and political upheavals of the mid- to late-1960s resulted in forever lowered levels of volunteerism, political participation, trust, and social cohesion among Baby Boomers.

And this is where Putnam leaves us: two idiosyncratic wars in two distinct periods in American history, one leading to civic renewal and the other resulting in a precipitous decline in social capital. I found this point of departure dissatisfying. *How* and *why* are shared experiences so important for social capital?

For my senior thesis at Occidental College, I set to find out. I traveled to the town of Ferndale, California (population 1430) to explore social capital. Altruism, honesty, associational involvement, and social networks are more common, more elevated, more frequent, and more dense in the small town compared to the big city. Although my modest study would not be capable of proving nationwide social capital trends, I reasoned that I might be able to document an instance or two of something telling about social capital that was being overlooked elsewhere.

Through dozens of in-depth interviews, I found that Putnam's generational change interpretation largely held up. When controlling for education and other demographic variables, the people I interviewed who were 62 and older tended to be more trusting, more engaged, more altruistic, and more community-minded. Conversely, people who were in the Baby Boomer age demographic were markedly less rich in social capital.

Except for a few outliers that could not be explained.

For example, I would travel to the outskirts of town and meet a relative hermit, who was not engaged in any clubs or associations, not a member of the civic WWII-generation, whose only forays into town were for groceries and the post office. And yet, when I asked him about his sense of community and trust in other people, he beamed and referenced two obscure dates, which I heard referenced over and over again during my interviews in Ferndale: 1955 and 1964.

For all Americans, the years 1955 and 1964 are significant: Rosa Parks and the Montgomery bus boycott, the Civil Rights Act and the Gulf of Tonkin Resolution.

For residents of Ferndale, California, these dates hold another significance entirely, outside the realm of experience for most of us but of utmost importance to them: major flooding.

Even though no one was killed and the flooding would hardly make a dent in the national consciousness at the time, these shared traumas were landmark experiences for the people who lived through them. Hundreds of people in the community were uprooted and many houses, businesses, and livelihoods were damaged or destroyed. Stories were warmly recalled of Joe at the lumber yard boarding up all the downtown shop windows, the firefighters rescuing a cat from a tree, Nancy opening up her home up the street for flooded-out neighbors to lodge in.

When I asked about trust, residents remembered the concerned faces and helpful neighbors, working together to rebuild. A half century later, when I asked what community means to them, residents *proffered* the flooding as an example of community.

On a separate research trip to study social capital in Coromandel Town, New Zealand (population 1437), I met a man who was extremely active in civic life, a member of numerous clubs, etc. By all indicators, he should have been an exemplary social capitalist. Except he was downright distrustful toward others and disparaging toward the town community. When I asked why he felt this way, he said that his house had been burglarized a few years ago. The perpetrators had never been found. The authorities were not helpful. The crime was probably committed by someone in the community, but the neighbors seemed to care less. As a result, he said that he could no longer look at people the same way anymore.

A small town flood without any casualties and a non-violent house burglary are not the same as a global war, a terrorist attack with thousands of casualties, or even a 500-year flood in a mid-sized city in the Midwest. And yet the scope and severity matter little if you are affected. Whatever their size or impact, shared traumatic events can make an indelible imprint on the lives of the people who experience them, for better or worse. Social capital can be forged by shared traumatic events.

1955 and 1964 are part of Ferndale's collective memory, perhaps akin to December 7, 1941, November 23, 1963, and September 11, 2001 in the American conscious—the outliers we experienced. These dates brought me to the University of Cambridge, the June 2008 Flood in Cedar Rapids, Iowa, and my drive to better understand how and why shared traumas can bring people together or tear people apart—and do something about it.

Thus, this book.

Acknowledgments

I owe tremendous thanks to the people in Cedar Rapids who shared their stories with me and gave of their time generously.

A special thanks to Beth Miller, Susan Davidson, Liz Hoskins, Alice Rogers, Lisa Kuzela, and Kara Trebil, who opened up many doors in the community, served as sounding boards as I learned about the flood and the city, and were strong sources of local support. A special thanks to the Carl & Mary Koehler History Center and its outstanding corps of volunteers for providing uninhibited access to extensive newspaper archives; *The Gazette* and Paul Jensen, Director of Photography, for permitting use of many stirring photographs; the City of Cedar Rapids GIS Department for permitting use of two flood maps; and Cornell College for access to its library. This project would not have been possible without my extended family in nearby Mount Vernon, and especially my aunt, Sally Farrington-Clute. Thank you.

At the University of Cambridge, I am grateful for the guidance of many scholars from the Faculty of Human, Social, and Political Science, especially Jackie Scott, my supervisor, and Jane Nolan. From St. Catharine's College, I'd like to thank the staff who supported me through the year, and to my generous benefactors for making sure that I could complete this manuscript. Erhardt Graeff,

Katrina Jurn, Edward Cohen, Hayley Darden, and Darci Palmer provided helpful input at different stages of this manuscript; their sagacious feedback is only eclipsed by their friendship.

A special thanks to my publishers for their patience and support, in particular Nicolette Amstutz at University Press of America, Julie Kirsch at Rowman & Littlefield, and the other editors with whom I have had the pleasure to work. I am also thankful for the wonderful folks at Taylor & Francis, for supporting this project. Portions of this manuscript have been adapted from a chapter in an earlier volume I wrote for Taylor & Francis, based on my research.

Finally, I am forever grateful for my dad Paul and brother Kristopher, who buoyed me. Dedicated to my mom, Joan Carol Farrington, who taught me that "people are people."

Part I

Chapter One

Introduction

WHY STUDY DISASTERS?

"Catastrophes are great educators of mankind," stated Harvard sociologist Pitirim Sorokin (1942, 10). They reveal much about the affected society. Normally latent social processes are "more visible in times of a disaster as they are compressed in a very dramatic and short time span," said disaster studies specialist Charles E. Fritz (1961). Because disasters disturb whole social systems and "break the cake of custom" of the pre-disaster form of life, a unique opportunity exists to investigate a social system's structural and cultural order (Fothergill 1998, 11). One can learn much about a society's underlying networks and norms by studying the disaster situation (Kalayjian 1999, 91).

Disasters further our understanding of complex social systems, as they expose where a society is vulnerable and where it is resilient. They inform policy because they suggest how societies might improve. Disasters, especially natural disasters,[1] have been one of the greatest forces on human life throughout its history. Among natural disasters, floods in particular have caused the greatest loss of life and property (Tufty 1978, 184).

The study of disasters is the study of societies: for without human vulnerabilities in organized social systems, there would be no such thing as a disaster.

WHY STUDY SOCIAL CAPITAL?

From economic performance to government effectiveness, crime to education to health and well-being, the societal benefits of social capital are vast and well-documented (Halpern 2005; Putnam 2000). To be sure, social capital is neither a "magic elixir" that cures all social troubles (Uslaner 2004) nor is it always beneficial for the greater good—organized crime, terrorism, and ethnic rivalries all depend on social capital to thrive (Warren 2008, 123).

Even so, communities marked by a high level of social capital— i.e., *resource advantages from social networks and norms*[2] tend to be more trusting, more civically and politically engaged, better providers of members' security and emotional needs, more philanthropic, and more efficient (McLean, Schultz, and Steger 2002, 1–6; Putnam 2000). On a top-down comparative basis, the study of social capital teaches us about relative levels of community health and well-being between different societies.

But social capital is *not* evenly distributed or equally felt. Although social capital is fundamentally a collective good, it is undoubtedly a highly stratified and differentiated resource that fissures along social and demographic fault lines. Access to and use of social capital is not equal between actors. In a bottom-up case study approach like the one employed in this book, the study of social capital—much like the study of disasters—reveals vulnerabilities and resiliencies concealed within a society.

INTERSECTING TWO RESEARCH CANONS

Little field research has examined the relationship between disasters and social capital (Wenger and James 1994, 230; Kaniasty and Norris 1999, 54). Even smaller is the canon that analyzes how social capital is impacted by natural disasters.

On the natural disaster side of the research divide, the reader must unearth social capital fluctuations from articles on the role of social capital in disaster response (Dynes 2002; Nakagawa and Shaw 2004) or from studies on a disaster's ability to decimate the general social order or to expose social structures and show them to be highly inequitable (Erikson 1979; Klinenberg 1994). All are related works, but do not have a direct focus on social capital and natural disasters. In the limited number of studies that focus directly on these two concepts, the emphasis is on social capital as an enabler of effective disaster response and group functionality in post-disaster society (Barnshaw and Trainor 2007, 95). The causal arrow runs from social capital as the independent variable to the disaster response and recovery as dependent variables.

On the social capital side, the cross-pollination between the two fields is even less so. In the rather brazenly titled *Handbook of Social Capital* (Castiglione, van Deth, and Wolleb 2008), for example, there is no entry in the index for the term *disaster*, *emergency*, or *crisis*. As a well-regarded 600-page work on social capital that offers, according to its Oxford University Press website, "a more considered and critical assessment" of various applications of social capital, this omission should be curious. Not because disaster studies has played a major role in applied social capital research, and therefore merits a place—but precisely because it has not.

The broader implications of disasters for community life demands further attention (Norris et al. 1994, 394).

THE CEDAR RAPIDS FLOOD OF 2008

The city of Cedar Rapids, the manufacturing capital of Iowa and the state's second largest city, experienced epic flooding from June 11th to 13th, 2008. The flood stage for the Cedar River is 12 feet, which snakes through the city and bisects it from east and west. During three of the city's worst flood years (in 1851, 1929, and 1993), the waters of the Cedar River reached approximately 20 feet, swelling the riverbanks and causing relatively minor amounts of damage. On June 13th, the Cedar River waters crested at 31.12 feet, approximately 20 feet above flood stage and an astonishing 11 feet higher than the previous record flood set in 1929 (see the maps in Appendix 2).

A confluence of meteorological events created this worst-case flood scenario (cf. Tufty 1978, 203). The previous winter had been particularly bad for Cedar Rapids. Sixty inches of snow fell, leaving the ground supersaturated and unable to absorb much water. Earlier in the week, heavy storms in Waterloo drained south into the Cedar Valley and Cedar River. Major rainfall soaked the city from Wednesday night until early Friday, including flash floods on Thursday the 12th. The waters crested at 10:15 a.m. on Friday the 13th.

Ten square miles of Cedar Rapids were flooded. More than four-thousand homes were destroyed. Eight to ten-thousand jobs were lost. Damage costs are estimated to exceed $1.5 billion (MCEER Information Service 2008). "It's just unbelievable," said Bess,[3] an 84-year-old resident who lived in a bungalow in the Time Check neighborhood for 65 years. "I mean it's still kind of like, 'this couldn't have happened.'"

OVERVIEW

This book analyzes *how* disasters impact social capital, and *why*. The June 2008 Flood in Cedar Rapids, Iowa, which crested at a record five feet over the 500-year flood level, provides a dynamic case study to explore in-depth the vastly under-explored link between natural disasters and social capital. By using a highly stratified and differentiated collective conceptualization of social capital, this book shows that residents' perceptions of social capital after a natural disaster are shaped by their vulnerabilities and buoyancies, which vary substantially and need to be understood contextually with scrutiny for detail and nuance.

Chapters 2–4 establish the necessary theoretical foundations to analyze how natural disasters impact social capital. In Chapter 2, I introduce an anthropogenic conceptualization of natural disasters that avoids *a priori* assumptions of what was *disastrous* and what was *natural* in the context of the Cedar Rapids flood.

Chapter 3 tackles the topic of social capital. A "clear orthodoxy" for understanding social capital is reached by finding common ground between the more private-focused view of Bourdieu and the public-focused view of Putnam.

In Chapter 4, I apply this framework on a hypothetical plane, which yield a conceptualization of social capital as a highly stratified and differentiated collective (rather than private) good.

Chapter 5 describes the flood and its aftermath, from the eyes of residents of Cedar Rapids who endured it. I consider respondents' perceptions on the physical impact, the local government response and recovery efforts, and the role of the wider Cedar Rapids community in the aftermath of the flood. All three are found to influence perceptions of social capital post- flood, which I investigate in the subsequent chapters.

In Chapter 6, I examine the central theme of this book: whether community in Cedar Rapids was strengthened or weakened by the flood. This discussion, framed under the themes of unity and change, demonstrates that the hardest-hit respondents tended to focus on the recovery and its associated problems, and were the most critical and cynical in their outlook of social capital. Less affected residents tended to focus more on the immediate response and the wider sense of togetherness that accompanied it.

In Chapter 7, I analyze why some respondents were harder-hit than others, and accordingly, were more negative in their views of social capital after the flood. I find that the flood was more disastrous for some residents than others based on an unevenness in their vulnerabilities and buoyancies going into the flood.

In Chapter 8, I find that respondents' accounts of social capital on many issues were less contradictory on closer scrutiny than first appeared. Changes in circumstances and disparities in condition are found to influence residents' perspectives of social capital postflood, rather than opposing world views or irreconcilable opinions on the same matters. I propose a framework comprised of four key interrelated factors that determined the current condition (and perspective) of respondents: background characteristics, structural aspects of social capital, cultural aspects of social capital, and the current, contextually-specific situation in Cedar Rapids. The loss of social networks, the durability of the "therapeutic community," and the fluidity of flood-related circumstances in Cedar Rapids are found to be especially important.

Chapter 9 concludes this book by noting limitations, suggesting avenues for future work, and highlighting the need for greater contextual specificity and incorporation of disaster studies into social capital research, and vice versa. Specific to Cedar Rapids, I summarize that with the advent of new problems over time, the condition of more vulnerable residents simply deteriorated while more buoyant residents maintained their deepened communal feelings as they returned to relative normalcy. How well a resident fared in the flood dictated whether they focused in conversation on the initial response or longer-term recovery efforts. Consequently, this preoccupation on either response or recovery determined their perspective on social capital and the general state of community after the flood.

An appendix follows that sets forth the methodological decisions that guided my fieldwork. Notably, I examine how a qualitative research design, centered on semi-structured interviews with flood victims and key informants, yielded the right combination of detail and flexibility for this exploratory study.

At the time I first left Cedar Rapids, about four months after the flood crested, the rebuilding and recovery process was still very much ongoing. Flood-affected residents continued to muck and gut their water-logged homes, unsure whether to stay or go. The local government deliberated the merits of various flood-prevention proposals involving levees, flood walls, green space, and river dredging. New flood-lines had not yet been set and more home buyouts were anticipated. All the while, residents waited nervously, wondering what the future would hold for Cedar Rapids and for themselves.

Four years on, when I returned and spoke with many of the same residents about their experiences with the flood and its aftermath, experiences varied considerably. Some described the progress since the disaster, specifically the revitalization of the downtown district and Czech Village, various businesses, and occasionally neighborhood blocks. Other residents focused on the losses: the evisceration of historic neighborhoods like Time Check, the lower-income residents who fled, the damaged trust in city officials and local institutions. All gone.

Whatever the focus or predicament, it was clear that the flood was a catalyst for unprecedented changes in Cedar Rapids in terms of its impact on trust, sense of togetherness, civic engagement, and other measures of social capital. The unsatisfying notion that "generational change" is the primary culprit for social capital shifts in society—popularized by Robert Putnam in *Bowling Alone*—does not explain what happened in this case study.

Instead, the outlines of a new theory emerge for how and why social capital shifts in societies from one generation to another: the transformative impact of shared traumas. In highlighting the enormous impact of one disaster in one mid-sized city in the Midwest, it is my hope that past and future disaster events—and in turn, social capital fluctuations in society—will be looked at anew.

Chapter Two

Natural Disasters

WHAT IS A NATURAL DISASTER?

The term "natural disaster" is problematic. It presumes that naturally-occurring forces have created an event that is inherently disastrous in terms of its effect on human systems (society and its internal processes) (Barton 1969; Drabek 1986). According to this classical interpretation, disasters are divisible into two exclusive categories: "either natural or manmade" (Ursano et al. 1994, 6).

But, as Quarantelli (1987, 14) proclaims, "There were no disasters before human beings evolved despite the cataclysmic physical upheavals in the evolution of the planet!" Disasters are not caused by natural hazards,[1] but by the confluence of natural hazards *and human vulnerabilities* (Rozario 2007, 16–22; Blaikie et al. 1994, 5–11). The burden of agency is on human societies, not God or Mother Nature, for "so long as the city resists the earth-shocks, so long as the levees hold, there is no disaster" (Dombrowsky 1998, 24 [Carr 1932, 211]). This interpretation introduces the role of humans in "causing" disasters, whereas the classical interpretation ignored it (Bolin, Jackson, and Crist 1998, 27).

Disasters are "the outcome of hazard and vulnerability coinciding," where hazards are, in this context, naturally-occurring phe-

11

nomena with the potential to harm individuals or human systems, and vulnerabilities are exposures to risk with the inability to avoid or absorb potential harm (Pelling 2003, 5). A disaster is the confluence of human vulnerabilities and natural hazards.

Natural hazards have the potential to harm some people and to have negligible, mixed, or even positive effects on others. Such uncertainty in the outcome is linked to varying degrees of vulnerabilities between various factors, including social, economic, and political processes, inequalities, demographics, protective mechanisms, and land use (Blaikie et al. 1994). Therefore, what we refer to as a natural disaster is neither intrinsically nor entirely disastrous—the social and physical disruption resulting from the event is what can be disastrous (Quarantelli 1985, 43–44).

Too few researchers have questioned the value-laden notion that "disasters, whatever they are, are *bad*" and are "negative events" (Quarantelli 1998, 265–266). As Quarantelli recommends, empiricism should come before assumption in regards to assessing a disaster's *disastrousness*.

Natural disasters are not purely *natural* either, because natural processes are increasingly anthropogenic. Human contributions to global warming through greenhouse gas emissions have increased the incidence and severity of floods and hurricanes (Picou and Marshall 2007, 9). An event such as Hurricane Katrina, which decimated New Orleans, was "caused" and made worse by an assortment of natural and very unnatural processes, involving loss of wetlands, levee breaches, topography, poverty, poor government planning and response, and global warming. Sifting out the *natural* portion from Katrina would be difficult.

Therefore, disasters are the outcome of human vulnerabilities converging with "natural" hazards, are only partially natural, and are not entirely disastrous.

Traditional periods of time within the course of a disaster are preparedness, response, recovery, and mitigation (Drabek 1986;

Fothergill 1998, 12). This case study concentrates on both the *response period*—which includes pre- and post-impact inventory of the situation and rescue (spontaneous, local, unorganized extrication, and first aid) and remedy (organized and professional relief)—and the *recovery period* (individual rehabilitation and readjustment; community restoration of property; the first returns to "normalcy") (Dynes 1970, 56–57).

Chapter Three

Social Capital

WHAT IS SOCIAL CAPITAL?

Vigorous debate without a clear consensus characterizes the attempt to precisely define *social capital*. Divisions persist on seemingly all aspects of social capital: how to measure it (Arneil 2006, 106), whether it is capital (Arrow 2000), whether it is possible to define (Arneil 2006, 117; Castiglione, van Deth, and Wolleb 2008, 9), and whether it is valid as a field of inquiry (Fine 2001, 13–15). Whether there should still be debates is also debated (Hooghe & Stolle 2003, 1).[1]

These debates serve an essential purpose. Until a basic framework is settled on and applied, the term risks suffering as all-encompassing and vacuous: trying to be everything and, as a result, lacking clarity and usefulness (Fine 2001, 12; Harriss 2001, 82–96). How a social scientist thinks about and defines social capital is not mere semantics: it is intrinsically connected to how social capital is measured and analyzed, and therefore is of utmost importance. Of course, contextual and discipline-specific conceptualizations of social capital are appropriate, even desirable (Foley, Edwards, and Diani 2001, 276).[2] However, a common core outline of "*what is social capital?*" eludes researchers, and is worth establishing.

Some believe that a fundamental outline already has been established but has not been adequately engaged or appreciated amid the wrangling (Halpern 2005, 31–39). Namely, social capital can be reduced to its two sets of constitutive parts: (1) structural and cultural aspects, and (2) private and public resources. Latent agreement towards this "clear orthodoxy" exists even in the otherwise incongruent conceptualizations of Bourdieu and Putnam (van Deth 2008).[3]

By concentrating on a specific set of theoretical agreements and divergences between Putnam and Bourdieu, a "clear orthodoxy" of "what is social capital?" can be established. This "clear orthodoxy" is not indicative of each scholar's full expostulation on the topic nor is it representative of all the major theories. Rather, the conceptualization is pragmatic: it provides the contrast and flexibility needed to analyze social capital through a qualitative community case study such as this one.

As an aid to further comprehension, the clear orthodoxy is applied on a hypothetical plane with an analogy of social capital to the Commons. The idea of the Commons encapsulates the framework of social capital surprisingly well. Taken together with a framework and conjectural application via the Commons analogy, social capital as a research scheme will be readied for functional use in the Cedar Rapids Flood of 2008.

THE STRUCTURAL AND CULTURAL ASPECTS

In their respective definitions, Bourdieu and Putnam split social capital into two distinct but interdependent components, the structural and the cultural:

- "Social capital is the sum of the *resources, actual or virtual*, that accrue to an individual or a group by virtue of possessing A

DURABLE NETWORK OF MORE OR LESS INSTITUTION-ALIZED RELATIONSHIPS of mutual acquaintance and recognition" (Bourdieu and Wacquant 1992, 119). [4]

- "Social capital refers to CONNECTIONS among individuals— SOCIAL NETWORKS and the *norms of reciprocity and trust-worthiness* that arise from them" (Putnam 2000, 19).

[*Italics* refer to cultural aspects; Text in ALL CAPS refer to structural aspects]

Both Bourdieu and Putnam embrace a conceptual distinction between structural and cultural aspects of social capital (van Deth 2008, 151–156). Other scholars have validated this structural/cultural dichotomy by adopting it with few modifications (Goddard 2003, 59–60; and Hooghe 2008, 572). Thus the following basic consensus emerges in how to think about social capital: a.) There are structural aspects to social capital, which include social networks and connections; b.) There are cultural aspects to social capital, which include norms (such as reciprocity and trustworthiness), as well as values and obligations; c.) Structural and cultural aspects are interdependent to some degree; and d.) Social capital cannot be understood without understanding the role of both aspects.

IS IT A PRIVATE OR PUBLIC GOOD?

Is social capital more of a private or public good? Bourdieu conceives social capital as symbolic but able to be converted into economic resources through private, networked ties. Putnam regards social capital to be a multi-purpose resource that arises from a discrete web of social connections that serve as a public resource. In the words of social capital scholar David Halpern (2005, 10), Putnam "has tended to frame the concept in terms of its public good aspects, explicitly including reference to the facilitation of cooperation, a definition that is sometimes sharply contrasted with Bourdieu's colder, more privatized definition."

Bourdieu conceptualized social capital as an economic resource that is accessed socially: a person has access to something of economic value through another person. That could be a recommendation for a job, or as we will see in this case study, knowledge of how to apply for emergency aid, information on pertinent flood recovery decisions, or familiarity with the law on such issues as price-gouging by landlords. In this interpretation, social capital is an element of distinction between individuals that is more of a private good (van Deth 2008, 151; McLean, Schultz, & Steger 2002, 6; Portes 1998).

For Bourdieu, social connections and relationships (the structural aspects) are means through which individuals, households, or small groups secure or are denied access to resources (the cultural aspects; Dudwick et al. 2006). Social capital exists in embedded relationships between individuals "more as personal assets than public goods" (Halpern 2005, 203). Inequalities develop within a social system that are derived from disparities among actors in the quantity and quality of ties, access to ties, intensity of use, and durability of network. Some have a head start in life, for social capital breaks across power lines and is not equally available to all (Bourdieu 1986, 243; Arneil 2006, 8; Horvat et al. 2003, 344; Kawachi and Berkman 2000, 177).

Putnam interprets social capital, first and foremost, as a public good that is the driver of community progress. Communities have social capital because intimate connections between residents create a large collective cache of social capital from which everyone can benefit. Putnam illustrates his bias for a public goods interpretation by overlooking requisite components of a privatized view of social capital: notably, he pays little heed to "the wider sweep of historical exclusion and assimilation" (Arneil 2006, 5). Putnam's focus is on how social capital breaks across environments and groups—one social system to the next—but not *within* social systems, often neglecting to ask *who is excluded or marginalized?* The benefits of social capital (and to Putnam, they are mostly *benefits*) reach all members of a social system—thus, the rising tide of social capital lifts all individual vessels.

A key difference between these two interpretations is over the question of whether social capital is "by definition available to each participant" or is "to be found in networks of individual participants" (van Deth 2008, 156). Problems exist with either view.

Putnam's trickle-down public view is assumptive and ahistorical—it assumes that all community members are on level footing in terms of access, opportunity, and social embeddedness. This view overlooks the *accumulated private benefits* of social capital hoarded by the critical mass—the power-yielding majority which must accept community-wide norms before they can be translated into social capital (Foley, Edwards, and Diani 2001, 269)—which peripheral members of society *cannot* access or utilize.

Conversely, Bourdieu's conceptualization of social capital, in its person-to-person networked approach of an individual's social relationships (Halpern 2005, 109), under-appreciates the *accrued public benefits* of social capital that a large portion of society (and not just the power-yielding and norm-setting majority) *can* access and use (Field 2008, 20).

An appropriate social capital framework should allow for the prospect of either interpretation, while noting each one's shortcomings. With this stipulation in mind, the following basic four-part framework for understanding social capital emerges:

1. *Social capital is comprised of two dimensions, structural aspects and cultural aspects. Structural aspects include social networks and connections. Cultural aspects include norms, values, and obligations. These two dimensions are more or less inter-dependent, and exist in what is best understood as*

one of two imperfect interpretations of social capital: as a private or public good.

2. *As a private good, resources are embedded between actors (individuals or groups) and are theoretically not available to actors outside a specific networked tie. This interpretation's shortcoming is that it rejects, a priori, that some effects of resources reach other actors through "spillover" from private social networks and/or synergy from the aggregate of private social networks in a society. As society is more than the sum of its parts, when summed together, new advantages and disadvantages may be commonly pooled that otherwise would not be felt.*

3. *As a public good, resources exist in a discrete web of social connections that forms a large collective cache of social capital theoretically available to all actors within a social system. This interpretation's shortcoming is it overlooks social capital differentiations within a society caused by variance in vulnerabilities and buoyancies between members. Parity does not exist in access to or use of resources. Understanding social capital as a public good risks being dismissive of the stratified, accumulated advantages and disadvantages in power and opportunity some actors possess over others.*

4. *Social capital is context-bound: it varies in each distinct setting and can only be understood by the characteristics and dynamics within a specific social system.* [5]

Chapter Four

An Analogy

SOCIAL CAPITAL AS THE COMMONS

The four-part social capital framework provides a strong conceptual starting point, but it is not sufficiently instructive for application when standing alone. Therefore, it is useful to think of social capital as *something* else to reach a workable meaning; something that encapsulates and processes the main claims of the above framework, and then fuses them together into an amalgamated, single cogent account; something that offers a setting in which gaps in access and use can be illuminated and explained; and something that addresses the many nuances expected within a social system. It is useful, therefore, to think of social capital as the Commons.

In the analogy that follows and throughout this book, Putnam is used as the approximate starting point for conceiving the social capital field, and Bourdieu for developing it. Here we start with the base assumption that, hypothetically, social capital is a collective good—a slight but not insignificant difference from labeling social capital as a public good because the former carries less of an assumption that social capital is available to all than the latter. Therefore, the social capital field is developed contextually from this collective good starting point and is found to be wrought full of inequalities and disparities.

Theoretically, everybody in a social system has equal access to and use of the Commons.[1] It is a shared public space where community members can come together, exchange information, make new connections, strengthen old bonds, establish values, and negotiate and decide norms (e.g., Is it safe to leave kids unattended in the Commons? How many hours should community members volunteer each week?). Under this interpretation, everyone can benefit from the Commons. It is a collective good.

Or is it? Does everybody in the community have equal access to the Commons? Is its use evenly distributed? Are the benefits common to all? Are all values, behaviors, and people welcomed?

The answer to all these, of course, is no. Despite the fact that, theoretically, the Commons is a collective good, everyone *does not* claim equal access or use. Power, privileges, and resource advantages concentrate among those whose access and use is highest. The Commons, like social capital, is a highly differentiated resource.[2]

Access and usability break across demographical lines, such as residential proximity to the public space (living five miles versus five blocks away), time and money constraints (a single mother of three working two jobs or a two-parent, financially comfortable family), and an assortment of health or physical-related issues (a paraplegic person versus a jogger).

These demographically-rooted inequalities in access and usability translate to inequalities in power. Each visit to the Commons brings another opportunity to strengthen ties with locals, receive valuable news, or expand one's social network. Over the course of multiple engagements with the Commons, these benefits accumulate and multiply. Regulars receive social resources that are advantageous in a social system. After a few weeks of visits, the well-off family of joggers that lives five blocks away might be invited by other regulars in the Commons to attend a barbecue or join a tennis league. Somewhere along the way, they become accepted members of the Commons' critical mass of people who, in turn, becomes the mainstay of the local community. All the while, the working mother that lives five miles away is left out.

Area of residency, socio-economic status, gender, health status, schools attended, and other demographical variables undoubtedly play a role in power accumulation and uneven access to and usage of social capital, as illustrated in this book. They constitute the first variable useful in determining an actor's advantages or disadvantages in a social system.

Inequalities created by the compatibility (or lack thereof) of an actor's *norms and values* with those of the wider society—the cultural aspects of social capital—are a second variable. A community member whose conduct is seen as at odds with the prevailing regulative norms of a community (i.e., the expected contributions to or performance in the system of the member) will be met with rejection and exclusion, even revulsion and disgust (Therborn 2002, 870).

Obedience is rewarded and distinction is not. A man who tries to join an ongoing football game wearing a cowboy hat and swimsuit is more likely to be met with ridicule and opposition than amiability. The critical mass may find these clothing choices unacceptable, and consequently reject this awkward cowboy himself. Some cultural or ethnic groups may also be treated differently, based on perceived normative incongruence. A North African male wearing a hooded djellaba would face additional scrutiny and hesitation from watchful parents than would a casually dressed Swedish woman. Snap assessments are made in regards to perceived normative behaviors and values.[3]

An actor's *social network* is a third variable that advantages social capital—its structural aspects. The likelihood that the djellaba-wearing man is welcomed is significantly amplified if a friend, who has already secured "the backing of the collectivity owned capital," vouches for him (Bourdieu 1986, 249). If the North African male was introduced first by a well-integrated regular in the Commons, his reception would be warmer. Alternatively, if he was accompanied by a distrusted outcast, the undesirable social status of this latter disrepute would be projected onto the newcomer.

Finally, access and use hinge on the current, contextually-specific situation in a society. Some norms and values take precedence over others at certain times, a fact that has very important implications for how disasters impact social capital. A minor faux pas that normally would ruffle some feathers is overlooked if a major prevailing norm has taken precedence and is being followed. If the man in the cowboy hat shows up at a massive pro-environment rally in the Commons wearing a Greenpeace sash too, it is safe to assume that his minor normative blunder (the "no cowboy hats" norm) will be tolerated as a result of his conformity to the major prevailing norm of the moment (environmental consciousness). During unique events such as a pro-environment rally (or a major flood), people who are perceived to hold different minor values and norms are more likely to be embraced, as a result of their emergent commonalities ("I guess that man in the cowboy hat is similar to me after all").

Like the Commons, access to and use of social capital is *unequal*, as measured by an actor's background characteristics, its cultural and structural aspects, and contextual circumstances and conditions. The result is a *collective version of social capital that is highly stratified and differentiated between actors and within a society*. In other words, it is the amalgamated form of social capital employed in this book.

An application of these definitions must be contextual: it must take note of both the unique characteristics and dynamics within the social system *pre-dating the disaster* and the current situation within the social system *influenced by or as a result of the disaster.*

The next chapter offers a streamlined local interpretation of the flood itself, the responses from the local government and the wider community, and lingering issues related to the long-term recovery.

Part II

Chapter Five

The Flood

A PERFECT STORM

On Wednesday, June 11th, 2008, Stephanie drove downtown to 500 First Street SE, where she works as a librarian for the Cedar Rapids Public Library. On this day, her commute was particularly bad— what normally was a 10 minute drive took 45. She watched the news that morning and "heard some roads were closed" but did not realize why.

By the time her shift began at noon, parts of 1st Avenue were already filling up with water. Less than 48 hours later, the 85,000 square foot library building was inundated and 185,000 items were destroyed in the largest public library disaster in U.S. history.

Stephanie started her day like tens of thousands of other Cedar Rapidians, totally unaware of the severity of what was to come over the coming hours, days, and months: "It was chaos [...] People didn't realize how bad it was getting. And it's really hard for people that don't live here to understand how little we understood about the flood." The flood was "way beyond expectations," confirmed Pamela, an official at the History Center. "The community was shocked," she said.

The ferocity of the waters shocked the local government, too. On Sunday, June 8, Alice, an elected county official, said that "we were still thinking in terms of a 20-, 22-foot flood crest." On Wednesday morning, the city's Emergency Operations Center was activated and a 24.7-foot crest was predicted. Mandatory evacuation of all people in the 500-year-flood-plain ensued. Water seeped up through storm sewers. Bridges were closed. Soon, the crest forecast gauge failed, "so we were kinda guessing at one point," said Beatrice, an elected city official.

On Thursday night, unseasonably heavy rains produced flash floods. Downtown Cedar Rapids and several neighborhoods were inundated, including Time Check, the Taylor Elementary School area, Czech Village, Oak Hill Jackson, and New Bohemia. Approximately 10,000 Cedar Rapidians were evacuated. A new, unthinkable crest would soon be reached: 31.12 feet.

In the dramatic words of Victor, an appointed city official, it was "the perfect storm" (see the maps in Appendix 2).

A PERFECT RESPONSE?

Without a single casualty or major injury from the flood, and very few cases of looting or burglary, residents expressed a mix of contentment and patience with the city's immediate response. "I think they tried ... Everything for the most part ran as smoothly as it possibly could," said Isabel, a lifelong Cedar Rapidian who works at Taylor Elementary School and is a leading advocate for the neighborhood. "I'm surprised what progress has been made; I think city officials have done a fine job" added Bess. "I think they did everything they could possibly do," said teacher and homeless advocate Zach, whose Oak Hill Jackson house was damaged by sewer waters during the flood. "I'm not into blaming individuals," declared Marion resident Quentin, who was involved in an initiative to collect positive flood stories from the flood. "There is plenty of blame to go around. But that's not the issue. Let's make sure it never happens again."

The overwhelming consensus among residents was that the flood was unpreventable, an "act of God" or "Mother Nature." They did not blame the city for any problems with the immediate response or the pre-flood preparedness. Jennifer, a homeowner in Time Check who has lived in Cedar Rapids all her life, remarked that "this was something nobody could guess." The flood was "way beyond expectations. I hope we don't see another one of these for 500 years," added Pamela, the History Center official. Olivia, an Oak Hill Jackson resident who had to vacate her house for months after it sustained major damage in the flood, put it succinctly: "the city did the best they could with what they were working with"—a flood of size and ferocity never before seen in Cedar Rapids and only scarcely imagined. "Nobody knew this could happen. Nobody," said Olivia.

Residents who focused on the city's immediate response were understanding and often laudatory. But not all residents focused on the response.

AN IMPERFECT RECOVERY

Interviewees who were still mucking, gutting, and waiting to return to their homes tended to focus on the city's longer-term recovery efforts, and were not so complimentary. "It's a mess," declared David.

In sharp contrast to the positive chorus of residents who described the city's immediate response ("they did the best they could with what they were working with"), mixed feelings and negative opinions abounded over the city government's longer-term recovery efforts. Three major criticisms of the recovery efforts were repeated: (1) the city has been slow in making decisions; (2) the city has been poor at communicating decisions and information on the ongoing planning process; and (3) the city has favored some groups and some areas over others.

Sluggish. Residents who were still rebuilding were especially frustrated with the city's sluggishness. Many of the victims I spoke with felt like they were "in limbo." David, a 61-year-old life-long resident in the Time Check area, lost his home, musical instruments, and recordings. House restoration projects remained on hold and antsy owners dared not sell in haste until the city decided which areas to buyout and where to draw new flood lines.

Michael and Nancy, a homeless couple living with two adolescent sons in a tent behind the abandoned home of a flooded-out relative, said they "just feel *stuck.*" The couple said they don't know what to do or where to turn for help. Michael has mental health problems and cannot keep a job, so the family has relied on Nancy's income and church friends to survive in the flood's aftermath. Cedar Rapids' low-income residents had the most riding on city actions, and thus were the most condemnatory towards city sluggishness and indecision.[1]

The floodwaters hit poor residents like David, Michael, and Nancy particularly hard. In a report entitled "Minorities, poor hit hard by flood," *The Gazette* confirmed that the flooded area of Cedar Rapids had general poverty rates (12.9%) that were about double those of the city as a whole (7.3%) and Linn County (6.3%). These figures are similar to the high percentage of minorities in the flood zone (12.4%) in a county where only 6.9% of residents are minorities (Smith 2008). The flood disproportionately affected the more vulnerable residents, as is often the case in a disaster period (Clarke 2006, 129).

Frustrated homeowners who were still "in limbo" said they felt anxious, upset, and generally skeptical of local government officials. Jennifer, a lifelong Cedar Rapidian, lost all confidence in the city government: "They can't seem to make decisions. I don't know if it's because they can't project into the future, or they are absolutely overwhelmed by the future." Her local church, St. Patrick's, was destroyed, and her Time Check home was flooded with 10 feet of water.

With the help of her nieces, Jennifer gutted and cleaned the water-logged first floor of her house. Even after the cleaning was complete, her house, which is at the edge of the 500-year flood plain, remained bare four months after the flood. If there was a buyout, she said she would sell; if there was not, she said she would wait. But, like so many others whose houses sustained major damage, her life remained on hold for months after the flood.

Edgar, a small business owner whose restaurant was flooded, was similarly frustrated: "The city council still hasn't made decisions as to what they are going to tear down, what they're going to buy, what they're going to allow to rebuild. There's still no hard decisions been made about what they're going to do with each area of the city." Edgar echoed these sentiments when we reconnected, four years later: "the house that was over there [across the street] they just tore down about three weeks ago and that's only because RAGBRAI [an annual bicycle race] decided they're coming through here ... so now they are getting a lot of that stuff down that needed to get done a long time ago." Edgar, Jennifer, and many other victims found the recovery efforts of the city government aggravatingly sluggish. "Now it's dragging out," concluded Pamela at the History Center.

Lack of Information. Many flooded-out residents displayed a high degree of confusion of what to expect next, as forcefully illustrated in the following exchange:

Clare, 56 years old, a resident of New Bohemia whose street was destroyed and family displaced by the flood, said: "You want to stop wasting the WD-40? They are going to tear all this down baby."

Her grandson Danny, aged 8, said: "If the city sees it all fixed up they might let us keep it. You want the city to take it? No! You just keep standing there talking."

Danny falsely assumed that a squeaky-clean cast-iron gate and a broom-swept walkway to his house would impress city officials enough to save it from its near certain fate of being razed. Although Clare forced a smile of resignation at the innocence of her grandson, Danny had highlighted a very important point with his comment: in contrast to the level of knowledge of city officials, the local newspaper (*The Gazette*), and residents who were less affected by the flood, flood victims tended to hold misinformed, hazy, or downright incorrect beliefs about what the city was planning, what was already planned, and what was yet to be decided.

The disparity between what was known and what was knowable reflects the social schisms in Cedar Rapids, running along fault lines of access and power. Without any ties to the city officials or access to fully reliable, up-to-date information, low-income residents such as David in Time Check, Michael and Nancy in Oak Hill Jackson, and 8-year old Danny and his family in New Bohemia relied on hearsay, assumptions, and the occasional newspaper report to predict what the city was planning to do and what would happen to their homes. According to Edgar, "there was no direction" from the city government on the eventual plan for buyouts: "there are a lot of houses that could have been saved if [residents] had been told there was going to be help ... so many businesses went out of business that could have been saved."

Favoritism. The city's alleged favoritism of some groups over others, especially downtown and businesses over homeowners and renters, was a third area of derision flood victims felt against the city in its handling of the recovery. Gloria, a renter in the Taylor School area who was displaced by the flood and lost her furniture and belongings, railed against the city's neglect of renters and the homeless. "They approve however many millions to rebuild the

Federal courthouse, but you've got people around here that still don't have a place to live, you know? Where's the priorities at here?"

When residents were asked what caused these problems, explanations ranged broadly: some said the city was narrow-sighted and not adequately prepared before the flood; others attributed the blame to kinks with the new system of government (changed by voters in 2005 from a commission to a weak mayor / strong city manager form). Some accused the city and local businesses of cronyism and still others lamented over perpetual ill-treatment and long-standing neglect of poorer neighborhoods. One particular criticism was repeated persistently: the task before the city was and still is enormous, and they have "no idea how to handle it." Fran, a 35-year old lifelong resident with two children attending Taylor, summed up this position: the local government is "clueless […] shooting by the hips of their pants as to what to do."

Everyone in Cedar Rapids seemed to describe the flood event as surprisingly huge. From this departure point, residents who sustained major damage to their home or work tended to focus on the city's recovery efforts (which were more likely to be criticized). Problems with the recovery disproportionately hurt them. Residents who did not experience extensive damage to their homes or who were able to move back to their homes within the first few months after the flood tended to focus on the city's initial response (which was more likely to be lauded). Residents' concerns reflected how the flood affected them individually.

THE COMMUNITY RESPONDS

Stirring examples of wider community involvement were shared often, usually with apparent gusto and pride. As Rebecca Solnit noted in *A Paradise Built in Hell,* "people often do best when they're [improvising] . . . it is when people deviate from the script

that exciting things happen" (Solnit 131). The story of how the last
city water well was saved is particularly symbolic. The story is a
fine illustration of civic action and the potentially facilitating role
of government (Dudwick et al. 2006). Alice, the elected county
official, provided the details:

> *I will never forget that call going out from the well fields, when
> we had one last well field. We had one guy from the city at the
> well field. He was the only one left there. He's like, "holy shit!"
> His radio was down and his cell phone was wet. Just happen-
> stance a couple of county guys come driving up in a truck. They
> actually still had a cell phone. They called down to the Emer-
> gency Operations Center. We put a call out, and that went on
> the media. And suddenly [...] it was like Field of Dreams. Re-
> member the end when all those lights are coming? That was
> exactly what happened! Here are these poor people, maybe four
> or five people trying to save this well field. And it's like, "Ah!
> The cavalry is coming!" And you see all these lights and all
> these people! People came out of the woodwork. Fifteen-hun-
> dred people... how insane is that? It's pouring rain. It's light-
> ning. You could be killed. [...] I saw the best and the worst in
> human nature [during the flood].*

The saving of the well, the last minute sandbagging and evacuation of Mercy Medical Center, and the Red Cross lunch wagons
driving through neighborhoods, doling out hot meals and drinks
and "Monterey Jack" sandwiches (as David enthusiastically remi-
nisced) were all offered as examples of Cedar Rapidians coming
together amid the tragedy. These touching moments became forma-
tive memories for both the flood victims and key informants I
spoke with in Cedar Rapids. "People saw more of a sense of community" in the aftermath of the flood, said Teresa, a volunteer
coordinator at Mount Mercy College. According to Norris et al.
(1994, 396), these types of post-disaster social activities may serve
to preserve both a sense of social embeddedness and the quality of
community life (396).

However, as Alice alluded to at the end of her remarks, some occasions of community misbehavior occurred as well. Fran, a flooded-out homeowner, decried the "greed" of the people, which she was shocked to see when she went to the Red Cross to collect clothes for her family and saw people taking much more than they possibly needed: "hordes of stuff," she said. A few stray stories of selfishness and disregard for others were offered: the Corvette show washing its fleet of cars at Lindale Mall in spite of city-wide orders for water conservation; occasional reports of looters breaking into flooded-out homes and stealing copper wiring and valuables; and one instance of a volunteer service provider financially exploiting its out-of-state Hispanic workers.

Even so, interviewees highlighted the rampant good over the isolated bad in discussing the community's behavior after the flood. After telling me about the greed at the Red Cross center, Fran was quick to mention that "it was total strangers that got us through it." She cited one example of a Cornell College fraternity that volunteered to paint her entire house, and completed the job in a single day as a result of eagerness and large numbers.

Volunteers from the local community played a major role in recovery efforts. Hammad, an imam,[2] told me how over ninety people came to help clean the Mother Mosque of America (the country's oldest mosque) after it was heavily damaged with 10.5 feet of water.

Retired Time Check resident Alan, who is 72 years old and has lived in Cedar Rapids for 68 years, shared the story of a mother who parked her car in front of his driveway with her young son in the passenger seat. The boy got out and approached Alan, carrying something in his arms. "Sorry about the floods," the young boy said, "here's some cookies."

These tender, resilient moments of shared humanity were the stories that came to mind when I asked residents whether the community was helpful after the flood, and whether the city and its citizens were going to pull together.

Residents who were better-off after the flood spoke highly of the efforts of the wider Cedar Rapids community in the aftermath of the flood, praising the helpfulness of strangers and fellow citizens. As neighbors were often unable to help out fellow neighbors as they faced similar predicaments, flooded-out residents looked further afield for support. Where church groups, extended friend networks, and other support providers stepped in to help, residents expressed greater optimism that the feelings of "we are all in this together" that were present by nearly all accounts in the immediate aftermath of the flood would endure.

Residents who were worse-off were far more likely to express feelings of isolation, neglect, and hopelessness.

Chapter Six

The Community

SOCIAL CAPITAL BEFORE THE FLOOD

Did the flood create a stronger sense of togetherness and community in Cedar Rapids? If so, will it last? If not, have the tensions between residents and the city over long-term recovery plans played a detrimental role? To understand how social capital was changed by the flood, the role of social capital and the structure of community life before the flood must be understood.

Neighborhoods in Cedar Rapids, while not comprising the total of one's social network, are its historical base. The older neighborhoods of the city were formed as ethnic enclaves and industrial offshoots. Blue-collar workers in Time Check crossed over the Railroad Bridge to work at the Quaker Oats plant each morning; residents with Czech and Slovak ties settled in Czech Village; and so on. Currently, these neighborhoods retain a strong sense of community, despite expansion, development, and dissection by major arteries. When interviewees were asked about the "sense of community" in Cedar Rapids, everyone mentioned the strength of community in the neighborhoods. In Cedar Rapids, neighbors are not just neighbors, they are circles of friends, confidantes, and often family.

Opinions varied as to whether a wider "sense of community" is present in Cedar Rapids, in addition to the agreed-upon sense of community in the neighborhoods. Many respondents said that divisions between neighborhoods of "blue collar" versus "white collar" fragmented the city, or at least kept it from being cohesive. "There has long been this line down Cedar Rapids that the river created, between the East and West side," said brothers William and Walter, founders of a service partnership that was recognized by local leaders, media, and residents as a significant player in the Time Check neighborhood rebuilding efforts.

Jennifer thinks there is a sense of community in Cedar Rapids. "I think there's the neighborhood, but I think there's a feel for the city as a whole." "Overall, there is a sense of community here," agreed Victor, an appointed city official, "and I think that it is exhibited by [...] some shared values within the community, shared history, and I think more recently—and I credit the city council for this—there's a shared vision for the community." The wider sense of community, according to respondents, comes in large part from the shared norms, values and experiences of Cedar Rapidians.

So what are these shared values and norms? Pamela said reciprocity and helpfulness. "There is an overall feeling of people helping each other, and strangers talking to each other." Xavier, the Taylor School official, believed trust was one. "Iowans and the Midwest are about that [trust]." Imam Hammad described Cedar Rapidians as people who "have principles." Other traits mentioned included self-started, independent-minded (i.e., not reliant on government), and genuinely nice.

Many interviewees mentioned a Midwest ethos or Iowan spirit that cherishes *hard-work* and *cooperative independence*, and has the effect of bringing people together. According to Edgar the restaurant owner, "Midwesterners have a can-do attitude. we're not going to give up." Residents relied on themselves as well as friends, neighbors, family, and other community members to help fix problems, rather than government handouts. This fact played an important role in the flood recovery as disparities emerged in a resident's ability to rebuild based on the size and quality of his or her social networks.

SOCIAL CAPITAL AFTER THE FLOOD

Regardless of whether they thought a strong sense of community existed before June 2008, the consensus (but not unanimity) among my interviewees was that the flood improved the sense of community in Cedar Rapids. Alice believes there is a chance now to realize a greater sense of togetherness by lessening the divides between neighborhoods, which was not possible before: "I think the recovery effort has an opportunity perhaps to blur some of those boundaries." Flood victim Bess agrees, saying that "the flood has been bringing a few people together. We are all in the same boat together, you might say. We have the same concerns. Sometimes it takes a disaster to do that." When asked how the flood affected community life in Cedar Rapids, most respondents answered like Bess did: the flood has brought the city together.

But Clare was doubtful. She recognized a general coming together of sorts "down in the main part of Cedar Rapids [...] they all joined in. Neighbors helped each other." However, Clare's block in New Bohemia was ravaged by the flood, a sad shell of a street now abandoned and waiting for city bulldozers to come. The wider community did not help. Her neighbors did not help, as they were too preoccupied with their own ruin to worry much about anyone else's. "[Over in this neighborhood] you kinda wonder where everyone left."

How did the flood affect Clare? *It tore my family apart. Mom, she only got 27 thousand for her home. The neighbor, he got 40 thousand [...] everybody went different ways. Like my brother, he*

*lived across the street. And mom, she's in her FEMA trailer now
[...] I moved in with my daughter [...] I feel like I'm just lost.*

Bess and Clare, both victims displaced by floodwaters, offered
two different accounts of community life after the flood. Bess bene-
fited from the strengthening of community, seeing it and personally
feeling it. Clare recognized a kind of general coming together, but
felt her neighborhood—her personal community, her own slice of
Cedar Rapids—was left out, tattered, and neglected. So, who was
right?

FOUR OUTLOOKS, TWO THEMES

Simple statements of "the flood improved the sense of community
in Cedar Rapids" or "the flood tore community apart" are vacuous
in isolation. Try to tell Clare that the flood improved the feeling of
togetherness in Cedar Rapids for everybody or, for contrast, say to
Imam Hammad that the ninety locals who volunteered to clean up
the Mother Mosque did not represent a strengthened community.

From the nuanced accounts of over 30 respondents, four core
outlooks materialize on how the flood affected community life. The
four outlooks were "we are all in the same boat together" and
"reevaluations will lead to social progress" on the more positive
side, and "some neighborhoods were decimated" and "new rifts
emerged" on the more negative side. From these four outlooks, two
evaluative themes emerged.

The first theme is unity. Is Cedar Rapids united? Most respondents thought so and pointed to the shared common experience of
the flood and reordered priorities of residents as proof. Residents
who disagreed or were conflicted about this wondered how the
community could be united while some neighborhoods lie in ruin
and many lower-income and minority residents continue to suffer
disproportionately from the flood, deepening social rifts along old
fault lines. Are all people truly in the same boat (read: situation)

together, or are some people worse off or better off than others? Do people feel that they are facing the same circumstances and challenges now? Can a flood improve social capital in a community for all?

The second theme is change. Unasked for change has come to the city in the form of a 31-foot flood. Further changes must follow as tough decisions are made in the recovery. The salient question becomes "what is positive change"? The majority of people interviewed expressed the view that "progress forward" was desirable and, they hoped, would be the lasting legacy of the flood. However, not all residents embraced the idea of forward change as progress. Will historical neighborhoods like Time Check and Czech Village be restored the same as before? What will change? Will city-wide changes be positive for everyone?

The themes of unity and change grapple with the most significant and controversial issues pertaining to how the floodwaters impacted community life. They seek to make sense of a mélange of seemingly contradictory feelings between and within my respondents as to whether the structural and cultural aspects of social capital were strengthened or weakened by the flood.

The majority of interviewees indicated the former—that the structural and cultural aspects of social capital were strengthened by the flood. These respondents tended to focus on the immediate aftermath and response. All key respondents and over half of my victims put forward some variation of the positive outlooks such as "we are all in the same boat together" and "reevaluations will lead to social progress."

The latter view, that the structural and cultural aspects of social capital were weakened by the flood, was advanced by a vocal minority that consisted of especially hard-hit, low-income victims who were still "in limbo" and a few informants who were likewise focused on the ongoing recovery and its many problems. These respondents tended to be highly critical of the city government, and doubted that the community could be strengthened amid decimated neighborhoods and escalating social rifts.

STRENGTHENED COMMUNITY:
WE ARE ALL IN THE SAME BOAT TOGETHER

Residents who believed that the flood brought about the feeling of togetherness and norms of helpfulness and trust in Cedar Rapids were overwhelmingly focused on the fact that the flood affected everyone in some way, directly or indirectly, and consequently had a unifying effect. The waters, they point out, did not discern between victims. All people suffered together "in the field" rather than "in the palace," analogized Imam Hammad. Differences of color and creed blurred as it became "vividly clear that we all are one when it comes to human needs of shelter, food, hopes, and the dreams. We all have the same."[1]

Olivia agreed, noticing a change in the city after the flood. "When you went to the department stores or went out in the floodway, people were affected, whether they were directly affected or indirectly. And our community was like, 'wow.' And so there was a lot of people—strangers—hugging ya." David saw the same phenomenon occur while waiting in long lines trying to get some assistance: "As much as you hated standing in lines, you had to break the boredom by talking." From these exchanges, "you'd almost feel like you knew them because they didn't live that far away and they had their own story, and it made you feel a wee bit better because you knew you weren't alone."

Norms regulating interaction eased—it became okay to just strike up a conversation with anyone if it began by talking about the flood. Echterling and Wylie (1999) wrote about the significance of these exchanges: "Because sharing stories necessarily involves others to hear them, the process helps to reconnect survivors, who may feel alone and alienated, to one another as they form a collective identity. The sharing of narratives also helps a community to gather individual experiences together to construct a mosaic of shared meanings of the disaster" (339). Through these casual but purposeful conversations, social networks grew and the sense of togetherness in Cedar Rapids increased.

For others, flood-centered conversations yielded valuable information that led to additional financial support, help from volunteers, and even future work contacts. "The relationships I've built working with people to find solutions, whether it be in my job or neighborhood, it would have taken ten to fifteen years or longer to establish those relationships. So when I look down the line in the future . . . you know, 'Are you really better and stronger from having this happening?' Yes," beamed Xavier.

As individual and societal needs merged, an ethos of helpfulness took center stage and the community united (Fritz 1961). "People just kind of joined together," recalled Gloria. "This city, because we have lost so much, people have really worked together," said Stephanie. Pamela also observed the cooperative spirit of residents: "Everybody seemed to pitch in and offer whatever was necessary . . . that's just what you do." Quentin remarked that "when things were at their worst . . . everyone was pulling in the same direction."

What is the effect of this coming together? "There are blessings to be had," said Olivia. "I think what it does is, people step back and they go 'well I have a lot; now I need to share.' And I think the community of Cedar Rapids has really done well with that. I really do." Teresa is also optimistic. She predicts community life will be even better than before in Cedar Rapids, more robust and with a more acute sense of civic pride. "Why?" I asked. "Because," she said, "we overcame this together, and we can do it." Because of the far-reaching devastation of the flood and the initial coming together of residents, the flood is a positive imprint that has "affected the hearts and minds" of all residents, concluded Imam Hammad.

As individual and societal needs merged, an ethos of helpfulness took center stage and the community united (Fritz 1961). "People just kind of joined together," recalled Gloria. "This city, because we have lost so much, people have really worked together," said Stephanie. Pamela also observed the cooperative spirit of residents: "Everybody seemed to pitch in and offer whatever was necessary . . . that's just what you do." Quentin remarked that "when things were at their worst . . . everyone was pulling in the same direction."

STRENGTHENED COMMUNITY: REEVALUATIONS WILL LEAD TO SOCIAL PROGRESS

Like any city, Cedar Rapids has its share of problems. According to respondents, these problems include lingering social divisions between Westside residents in lower-income neighborhoods and the more affluent residents in the Eastside; antipathy toward development and reluctance to embrace any kind of change; and an aversion toward dealing with anything contentious. "We tend to not want to talk about dissension. It used to be called the Parlor City . . . it's like, no conflict," said Rose.

These problems have produced a city that is, in the words of more critical respondents, "conservative," without much of a financial base, unattractive to young professionals, "depressed," and generally "stuck." An influx of new residents, the redevelopment of downtown, and the cultivation of the river "into an asset" are some of the cornerstones of these residents' push to address these alleged problems and progress forward.

According to Jennifer and the majority of the residents I met, the flood has "opened some doors" for positive change through reevaluations. "Now's the time to revitalize this place that got devastated," said Xavier.

Reevaluation occurs at the individual level with personal reflection on values and priorities (Ursano et al. 1994). Olivia discussed the changes that she made in her life after the flood: "The flood has made me really step back and take some inventory. And I've got a couple of home girls I love dearly—one in particular just wants to play victim all the time. You find that, with losing everything . . . you grow up a lot and you change a lot. And you do leave people behind . . . I look at some people and say, 'You know what? Get a life.'" Quentin professed that the most significant influence of the flood on him was "how I am living my life and how I can help others." Even if you were only indirectly affected, the flood "gave you a little of taste of not taking things for granted," said Rose.

The potential for change is palpable at the community level. The flood brought long-standing social problems to the forefront, including stigmas attached to some groups and inequalities in access and power between people. Olivia thinks the flood "calls people to really examine some things [in the community] that were broken, because the floodwaters exposed it." Alice similarly sees an opportunity at hand because leaders from different backgrounds can work together on long-term plans, perhaps lessening the class-consciousness of the city. Teresa agrees: "In the long run I think—maybe my hope, but also my thought—it will strengthen the sense of commitment to community and the resolve to overcome problems."

These respondents said that the flood will serve as a wake-up call. Problems and disparities exist that require attention and involvement from residents. "I think people had gotten really complacent. The city in general was complacent. And I think people in the neighborhoods were complacent. I think the flood was an awakening. . . . Some people realized that they needed to become more involved and active in their communities," said Isabel. According to Alice, social changes will last because the community's achievement requires its participation and collaboration. The community came together after the flood, operating under the mantle "we can work together, we are all in this together, we all have a responsibility for each other . . . this is our city," said Teresa. "It will be the great catalyst, or we're gonna get stuck again. And I don't know which yet," said Rose.

Most interviewees anticipated that the community will be more grateful, more altruistic, and more united in post-flood Cedar Rapids. Xavier foresees the community becoming all of these. "We are going to appreciate each other a little bit more, and give of ourselves, instead of 'what are you going to give to me?' 'what do I have to offer?' . . . when you've gone through a disaster like this, you can't hit much more rock bottom . . . you know, I'm not saying utopia or something, but you've got to pull together."

Because of the enormity of the event and its all-encompassing influence as a potentially "great catalyst," as Rose aptly put it, norms of reciprocity and togetherness prevailed after the flood. Social capital was strengthened in Cedar Rapids and the city continued to move forward together, according to most respondents (cf. Kalayjian 1999, 99).

WEAKENED COMMUNITY:
NEIGHBORHOODS WERE DECIMATED

"There are communities that are no longer in existence," reported Edgar the restaurateur. Neighborhoods like New Bohemia, Czech Village, and Time Check were obliterated. These low-lying areas near the Cedar River were older and lower-income neighborhoods and were disproportionately affected by the flood.

For support, residents from these neighborhoods tend to rely on social networks of friends, relatives, colleagues, fellow worshipers from church, and neighbors. These are ties to people from roughly the same socioeconomic stratum, not powerful elites who can provide valuable information or help. In one illuminating instance,

Gloria did not know which flood-affected items in her apartment could be cleaned and kept and which ones should be thrown away. She did not know whom to ask or how to find out. She was unaware of her own lack of access to potential help. Her young son has asthma, so Gloria did not want to take any chances and threw out almost all of her furniture. She absorbed a tough financial hit that could have been minimized if she had links to the right people who could have provided her with information on what was salvageable.

In terms of actual physical damage and exploitation of vulnerabilities, the flood hit lower-income areas the hardest. In the Taylor School area, where Gloria lives, nearly all houses were severely damaged and all the neighbors were uprooted. As Norris et al. (1994, 393) forewarned, "the people typically counted on for support in times of crisis may be victims themselves and unable to offer help." Precious social networks collapsed in these already-vulnerable neighborhoods, leaving residents greatly impaired by setbacks in the recovery. Residents continue to wait, rebuild, or flee as their chances to return remain uncertain.

Unscrupulous property speculators have been buying up homes for pennies on the dollar, offering quick cash to frustrated homeowners who are either misinformed or fearful about the ramifications of city buyouts or redrawn flood-lines in their local area. Lawrence, a community leader in the Northwest, loathes these opportunists and believes they are escalating the tragic destruction of the neighborhoods. He said the flood initially "renewed my faith in mankind, because people were reaching out to help." All of that has changed now:

> *Eight or ten weeks ago I thought, "what a great world we live in. You know, people are willing to give up their own time and energy and money." And then I see the other element come out [...] so how did it affect the neighborhood? It destroyed the neighborhood. It destroyed the people's hope. It destroyed their sense of belonging. It made them angry. It broke their hearts.*

There are very few stories that I could say to you that have a great deal of hope in them.

Interviewees from these historic neighborhoods offered many reasons why their fellow residents were choosing not to return. In addition to the administrative hurdles of trying to rebuild, respondents said that they were tired of the hassle of it all, scared about further property depreciation, and fretful that other neighbors will not return, leading to neighborhood decay. Walter lost his house in the flood and is nervous to return: "and frankly, I would love to. . . . There's a part of me that would love to move back into my house and be done with it all right now, if it weren't for the fact that half the houses around me are abandoned right now."

In Time Check, homeowners were able to point at each house on the block and tell the story of its occupant: rebuilding, sold to an opportunistic speculator ("vultures," in the eyes of Lawrence), abandoned, or waiting. They worried that such variance will cause the neighborhoods to deteriorate and create tension between neighbors. As Bess experienced, if one resident goes through a great deal of expense to use professional help in rebuilding, another spends the minimum on basic recovery, a third sells to a landlord who does little upkeep, and a fourth abandons, the first homeowner will understandably be upset and "might feel a little like they might have done too much, and the neighbors didn't do enough."[2]

The partial destruction of Cedar Rapids' neighborhoods—the historic base of community life in the city—displaced residents, damaged social networks, and blighted the face of the city, perhaps irrevocably. Imam Hammad misses his neighborhood. "It was a live community. 'Hey George! Hey Philip! Hey Lisa! Hey!' you know I mean, everybody talking. But now, nobody's there. I am sorry." As a result of the flood, neighborhoods in Cedar Rapids were decimated and, as residents of these areas fear, they will never be the same again. "Cedar Rapids isn't going to be the same for a long time. It's going to take us all working together to bring it back to some sense of normalcy," said Isabel.

WEAKENED COMMUNITY: NEW RIFTS EMERGED

Some of the worst-affected flood victims in this study's sample related something that was diametrically at odds with what was said by less-affected victims and informants: in relative terms, not everyone was affected by the flood. Severity varied dramatically, based on the physical impact and pre-flood vulnerabilities (or buoyancies), including socioeconomic status and size, quality, and intactness of social networks.

Gloria was particularly hard-hit. As a low-income renter with three kids of ages from six to eleven, her salary of less than $30,000 a year was barely enough to get by even before her apartment was flooded. She thinks it is hard for others to understand her condition. "If it wasn't your house or you didn't see it, you don't understand fully until you're in that situation. You probably couldn't imagine going into a house that is full of water and everything is just ruined. Until you see it. . . . I mean, that's their whole life." Even when Gloria remarked on how the community came together ("a lot of people that were *not affected by the floods* still came out and helped people clean out their houses" [emphasis added]) she described these people as "not affected by the floods" rather than less affected by the floods. According to Gloria, not everyone in Cedar Rapids was affected by the floods.

Edgar agreed that there is a disparity between residents who were hard-hit and members of the community who were either less affected, "not affected," or were somehow less vulnerable. "If you weren't affected, you don't quite understand what it's . . . and I don't understand even people that lost their homes. I mean, they lost all their mementos, and pictures, and things like that that are irreplaceable. All I lost was equipment here, you know. So I even probably have trouble empathizing with people who lost all that stuff."

David described the rift between these divergent groups in simple terms: "There's basically two types of people: the people that were affected and say 'I know how it is and I want to help no matter what.' And there's other people that say, 'Well I wasn't affected so to hell with it.' And that's really wrong." Michael and Nancy, the homeless couple, expressed similar anger over the fact that people were solely "focused on their own thing." The disaster, according to them, did not improve the sense of community."

According to the most hard-hit respondents, the numerous rifts that were created or made worse by the flood impinged on the sense of community in Cedar Rapids. In addition to the schisms mentioned earlier between the city government and residents, downtown business owners and residents, and homeowners and renters, new divisions arose between neighbors due to sizable differences in FEMA money allocations between flooded-out residents and "gawkers" touring ravaged areas and between the local media and residents who felt slighted by a lack of media coverage ("There is life over the bridge, you know?" complained Clare. "They never showed Taylor," said a disappointed Xavier).

The disaster seems to have "force[d] open fault lines that once ran silently through the structure of the larger community," thereby dividing Cedar Rapids into divisive fragments and weakening social capital, according to a vocal minority of my respondents (Erikson 1994; Nakagawa and Shaw 2004).

Part III

Chapter Seven

Two Cities?

The story of the flood came to me as thirty individual tales, each one distinctive. Some respondents focused on positives with the initial response; others focused on problems with the longer-term recovery. Some raved that the flood brought the community together; others said that there were now literally less fellow neighbors to be brought together, as neighborhoods were obliterated. Concepts recurred and themes emerged, but seemingly incontrovertible divides left the accounts of some residents at odds with others.

However, on closer scrutiny, the accounts of most residents do not seem as much at-odds with each other as they appear to be concentrated in two different points in time. Barring a few clear disagreements over specific topics, residents mainly focused on different aspects of the same matters.

For instance, when asked "how well did the local government do in handling the flood and its aftermath?" some residents replied by talking about the immediate response effort, the flood, which, the consensus was, was good. "I'm surprised what progress has been made; I think city officials have done a fine job," said Bess. "I think they tried . . . everything for the most part ran as smoothly as it possibly could," said Isabel. "I think they did the best they could with what they were working with," said Olivia.

When this same question was asked of other residents, they focused on the recovery efforts and the aftermath, which have been marred by setbacks. "They can't seem to make decisions. I don't know if it's because they can't project into the future, or they are absolutely overwhelmed by the future," said Jennifer. "I don't think they did well at all. And they're still not," said Gloria. "It's a mess," said David.

When asked about government performance, why did some residents focus on the response, while others focused on the recovery? If a resident first focused on the city's response and was later broached about the recovery, would his or her account of the recovery be consistent with that of other residents who focused first on the recovery (and vice versa)? Quite often, this was the case. When Jennifer, who focused on criticisms regarding the recovery when discussing the city government, was asked about the city's initial response, she displayed patience and understanding: "Nobody could have guessed this. The city should have done something with their levee. But it wouldn't stop this water. It was coming no matter what. This was just something nobody could guess." David was also tolerant toward the city's response. He thought the city government had tried its best, regardless of blunders. When asked if the city should be blamed for those blunders, he refused: "I would not go that far out on that diving board to say that people deserve to be blamed."

Despite their displaced status, difficult ordeals, and predominant focus on the flaws of the city's recovery efforts, David and Jennifer were both conciliatory toward the city's response efforts. By drawing out these nuances, the city described by Jennifer and David begins to look similar that described by Bess, Isabel, and Olivia, despite their differences in focus.

Why did some residents focus on the response while others focused on the recovery? The answer lies with Gloria and the idea of vulnerabilities. Unlike Jennifer and David, who also criticized the government's role in handling the recovery, Gloria did not give an ounce of credit to the city government (or the federal government for that matter: "they were even worse"). Her focus was entirely on her own ongoing plight as part of the recovery. Anything that made her struggle worse was condemned:

> *I've been applying for rental assistance through FEMA since July 1. I've now faxed them 23 different pieces of paper. Half the time I can't get through on the phone with them. I've been out to their office probably five times on Westdale [Mall]. Nobody knows anything [...] I can't stand that place. I don't know how they went about deciding who got this amount and who got that amount, but it wasn't right [...] I don't know who to call [...] a friend of mine who got flooded out—she was applying for the same assistance—and she just gave up. She said, "I'm just not going to do it anymore." And I think that's what they want you to do. They make it so hard that you'll just say, "forget it." But I'm not going to leave them alone, 'cause I can't afford to right now.*

Anything that improved her lot was cherished:

> *People just kind of joined together. They've helped other people in different ways: donating clothes or their time ... I even had a lady in Walgreens—I was in a line getting a prescription, this is not too long after the floods—and she said "I have Boy Scouts— a son in Boy Scouts. And these boys want to do whatever they can." And she took down my number and she said, "they'll help you move your stuff out. They just want to get in and help somewhere and in some way."*

Gloria was entirely focused on her present situation because it demanded her entire attention. She focused on the government recovery because that was what impacted her right now. Thinking about the city's response would have been irrelevant—a distant memory at best that would not fix her current financial and emotional plight.

Gloria is a low-income renter in the Taylor School area. As a young mother of three children who is unemployed and does not have a college degree, Gloria was just barely getting by before the flood. When the flood hit, Gloria took refuge in her sister's one-bedroom apartment. She stayed there with seven other people until July 1. She then moved into a new apartment out of desperation. Her decision was hasty, and now she is stuck in a $700 a month apartment "plus bills" that she cannot afford. Before the flood, she paid $500 and "no bills." Her attempts to secure assistance and information from FEMA and the local government have been futile, she says, "there's no help with, you know like I said, getting your rent paid or having help paying your rent. I'm sure I'm not the only one who took a place who can't afford it. So what's going to happen when people can't pay their rent in town?"

The flood was particularly disastrous for Gloria because she was particularly vulnerable. On an individual level, Gloria's background characteristics put her at risk. Gloria suffered from time and money constraints. She was without a job and without much of an education. Her priorities were her three kids and their schooling, which was complicated by the flood because they all attended Taylor Elementary, the only school in Cedar Rapids that was closed for the academic year because of flood damage. As we discovered about social capital in the Commons analogy, power and resource advantages "concentrate among those whose access and usage is highest" and "break across demographical lines." On both of these fronts, Gloria was particularly susceptible to disaster.

On a collective level, Gloria's degree of vulnerability was mixed. When asked what she likes best about living in Cedar Rapids, Gloria said, "my whole family is here. And I just know everybody. Know where everything is. People are generally pretty nice." Gloria was buoyed by an extensive family network, including a sister who took her in for 18 days after the flood. Gloria thought the flood improved the feeling of togetherness in Cedar Rapids: "a lot of people that were not affected by the floods still came out and helped people clean out their houses, or whatever they needed help with. I think it brought a lot of people together."

However, the flood destroyed the community as she knew it. Gloria considered the sense of community to be "more just in your neighborhoods, not as a whole." The neighborhood formed the base of community life in Gloria's Cedar Rapids, but she did not receive any help from her neighbors after the flood because her neighborhood was destroyed: "they were in the same boat as me, so to say." She lost her confidence in the government, which she said has been unresponsive and unhelpful and did not have an interest in her interests, favoring downtown businesses and homeowners over people in her situation. "I think the homeowners are the only ones that they're helping now . . . and, you know, the renters . . . well, just find another place and figure it out."

Even though Gloria felt that the sense of solidarity was high right after the flood, at that moment, her own world was teetering on the brink. When asked what she would personally remember most about the flood, her answer was illuminating in its restraint. Although most respondents recounted moments of heroism or particular heartbreak, Gloria could not look past the sheer physical magnitude of it all: "Just the whole thing. . . . I mean, all the water . . . and how much it ruined . . . it destroyed . . . and after the floods, the piles and piles of garbage. It just looked like a war in some areas." Her focus was entirely on the recovery efforts and not the response because the recovery efforts were relevant to her in the present. Out of sheer necessity, Gloria's focus was transfixed entirely on her ongoing plight.

As seen in the case of Gloria, there appears to be a basic four-part formula for deducing the views of a resident with regards to social capital after the flood: (1) the vulnerabilities of each resident vary, (2) and so varies the flood's degree of disastrousness for them, (3) and so varies their current focus on the recovery or the response, (4) and so varies their outlook on community life and social capital. Cedar Rapids is one city, albeit one that is highly stratified and differentiated. Vast discrepancies exist in the residents' vulnerabilities, leaving flood survivors at vastly different points in the recovery process. The flood was more of a disaster for some residents than for others based on their vulnerabilities.

But why were some residents more vulnerable than others?

Chapter Eight

One Framework

We defined vulnerabilities as "exposures to risk with the inability to avoid or absorb potential harm" from a natural hazard (Pelling 2003, 5). For a variety of reasons, residents of Cedar Rapids had different exposures to risk. We can identify these reasons and fully answer our question "why was the perception of social capital different for different people?" by recalling our analogy of social capital to the Commons. In that analogy, four variables were listed as determining an actor's advantages or disadvantages in a social system—essentially, an actor's buoyancies or vulnerabilities: (1) background characteristics, (2) structural aspects of social capital, (3) cultural aspects of social capital, and (4) the current, contextually specific situation in a society.

BACKGROUND CHARACTERISTICS

Background characteristics and demographics are important, as exemplified by the case of Gloria. Her unemployment, lack of a college education, time constraints as a young mother with three children, and low socioeconomic status left her particularly vulnerable (cf. Lin 2001, 58). Furthermore, Gloria lacked the knowledge and experience in using systems to apply for financial support or to gain information that could have both saved her a lot of money in salvaging some of her furniture and granted her great reprieve in her stress (she said her health was only fair based on mental anxiety).

STRUCTURAL ASPECTS OF SOCIAL CAPITAL

A second variable influencing power accumulation and advantage are social networks and connections—the structural aspects of social capital. To compensate for her demographic vulnerabilities, Gloria relied on her extensive social network of family and neighbors to endure the tough times. However, this network was disrupted by the flood as her neighborhood was decimated. A resident's ability to rebuild quickly was buttressed by preexisting social networks that were strong and still intact (Nakagawa and Shaw 2004). Alan thanked God for his friends and family, especially for his sons in the pipe-fitting and plumbing trades. He said his neighbors who were not as fortunate in terms of the quality or quantity of their social networks lacked money and could not rebuild.

Rose reported a similar phenomenon: "The employees who I've talked to who have been able to at least partially recover from the floods had family/employer networks." When I asked Yvonne, the flood coordinator at Rose's church in Marion, what allows some people to rebuild their houses faster than the others, she summed up the importance of the structural aspects of social capital:

> *I think resources. Not only just the financial resources, but if a person is plugged into the community and they have family or friends or co-workers that have really come in and helped, that's really been essential. But if someone isn't connected in the community, and they don't have the resources that their employers can give them, or friends and family, then they're the ones that just aren't far along at all.*

Rose reported a similar phenomenon: "The employees who I've talked to who have been able to at least partially recover from the floods had family/employer networks." When I asked Yvonne, the flood coordinator at Rose's church in Marion, what allows some people to rebuild their houses faster than the others, she summed up the importance of the structural aspects of social capital. "I think resources. Not only just the financial resources, but if a person is plugged into the community and they have family or friends or co-workers that have really come in and helped, that's really been essential. But if someone isn't connected in the community, and they don't have the resources that their employers can give them, or friends and family, then they're the ones that just aren't far along at all." As public policy professor Daniel Aldrich has observed from his research of Hurricane Katrina in New Orleans, the 2004 Indian Ocean Tsunami, and other disasters, "during and after a disaster, neighborhoods with deeper reservoirs of social capital can recover more effectively, efficiently, and quickly," in large part due to their ability to connect with authorities, spread information, and under-take collective action (Aldrich 2012). "Social infrastructure is at least, if not more, important, than sandbags, tents, and evacuation plans."

CULTURAL ASPECTS OF SOCIAL CAPITAL

The cultural aspects of social capital are a third variable that af-fected how well or poorly residents endured the flood. Norms, val-ues, and obligations served as a type of collective buoyancy, sup-porting many flood victims. All of my interviewees reported feel-ing connected with their fellow Cedar Rapidians right after the flood in ways scarcely imaginable beforehand. The variance was not so much in this experience—nearly everyone described a great-er normative sense of togetherness—but rather in a resident's cur-rent concentration. Recall that Lawrence, who focused almost ex-clusively on the decimation of the neighborhoods and negligence by the city in the recovery, initially felt that a greater value was placed on the community. He witnessed the norms of altruism and helpfulness emerge as the less-affected assisted the harder-hit:

> *My pastor at church asked me to write a little letter for the church paper, and said they wanted to know how the flood affected me (but not my house). And I said, well, at that time—this was 8 or 10 weeks ago—I said it renewed my faith in mankind, because people were reaching out to help. But shortly after that [...] 8 or 10 weeks ago I thought, "what a great world we live in. You know, people are willing to give up their own time and energy and money." And then I see the other element come out . . .*

The heightened sense of togetherness that occurred initially after the Cedar Rapids flood is an example of the therapeutic community. The therapeutic community is the period of elevated social capital utilization and expansion that often is reported immediately after a natural disaster (Dynes 2002, 41; Fritz 1961, 692). People in Cedar Rapids felt a greater sense of community because there was a greater sense of community. According to Kaniasty and Norris (1995, 165), "the sudden, unambiguous, and visibly distressing nature of disasters frequently invokes high levels of unsolicited help and spontaneous goodwill." In a therapeutic community, helping is contagious; residents notice fellow residents helping and feel obliged to contribute (Dynes 1970, 95). All attention is focused on the community's survival and recovery. Normal community functions become service oriented (Quarantelli and Dynes 1985). Outlets develop for communicating grievances. In effect, the therapeutic community is a type of idealized community; "we" takes precedence over "me."

In the analogy of the Commons, we saw that inequalities are created by the perceived incompatibility of an actor's norms and values with those of the wider society. However, in some instances, such as in the therapeutic community, the prevailing regulative norms of a community are eased and barriers are lowered to be welcomed into the wider community. As expectations change, the expected contributions to or performance in the system of a member also changes (Therborn 2002, 870). During unique events like floods, expectations for behavior change as civic norms and values take precedence over more independent-minded "live and let live" sentiments (Fischer 1998, 18). The result is a more cohesive sense of togetherness—a more therapeutic community.

The therapeutic community does not exist for everybody. Much like the "normal" community it is modeled after, the therapeutic community does not distribute aid "randomly or equally" (Kaniasty and Norris 1999, 32). Residents with larger social networks, better education, and higher socioeconomic statuses are favored (Kaniasty and Norris 1999). As we recall from our earlier definition, disasters reveal social processes and do not create entire new sets. "Patterns of neglect" differentiate social capital within a society even during times of disaster—perhaps less widely so than usual but all-the-more damaging for neglected residents (Kaniasty and Norris 1999).

The therapeutic community cannot be sustained (Fritz 1961, 690). As the situation of most residents improves or stabilizes, they no longer need the therapeutic community. It no longer affects them. Norms that had demanded the buoyant residents help the vulnerable ones will ease, and so the outlet for helping behaviors (i.e., the therapeutic community) is no longer needed because residents feel less urge to help out. Many flood-affected residents are able to recover and no longer need to receive much or any help. The therapeutic community cannot be sustained out of whim or desire; it appears out of sheer necessity in times of severe danger. When that time has passed for the majority of people, the therapeutic community disintegrates.

The respondents who rebuilt quickly or were less affected by the flood spoke in mainly positive terms about the city and community life. They were still enjoying the "amplified rebound" effect from the therapeutic community (Barton 1969, 279). Their well-being was no longer in jeopardy. Because the disaster was more of a relic of the past for them, they had the luxury of reminiscing about and memorializing the positives that came from the disaster in the form of the therapeutic community. In other words, the heightened civic state left its residue on more buoyant residents and became "a benchmark experience" by which social norms and opinions were shaped (Alexander 1993, 555).

Conversely, residents still mucking and gutting their homes lost the feeling of "we" taking precedence over "me" as they continued to struggle to survive. What was gained was now forgotten or viewed longingly, as something of a mirage: "there was a lot of help back then, and I needed it—I still need it, but now it is gone and I am on my own. Early on there was really a feeling of 'we are all in this together,'" said Walter, who lost his house and is still displaced. "But as the summer wore on, there was definitely people focusing more on their neighborhood . . . it felt like people over there [on the other side of town] were just having a normal summer."

If "victimization experiences" are indeed the "most direct way for people to verify their expectations that help would be available if needed," then residents who are still rebuilding are likely to maintain low expectations (Kaniasty and Norris 1999, 34). The predicaments of residents such as Gloria necessitate help, but less help is available or given, so many toil alone, focused solely on staying afloat. Kaniasty and Norris (1999, 41) found that "the initial mobilization of social support is sufficient to conquer neither the immediate nor the delayed deterioration in personal and community relationship." Timely community recovery for all victims after a disaster is not assured, regardless of whether the therapeutic community emerges, endures, or fades away.

THE CURRENT, CONTEXTUALLY-SPECIFIC SITUATION

The current context and circumstances in Cedar Rapids is a fourth variable to consider in rationalizing residents' perceptions of social capital. Opinions are not static. They are fluid, rising and falling with changing circumstances. If Lawrence was interviewed eight weeks earlier, he would have offered a very different impression of the flood and aftermath. His words would be appearing under sections like "we are all in the same boat" and "reevaluations will lead to social progress," not "some neighborhoods were decimated." The interview with Lawrence is an artifact in time, as are the other 27 interviews with his fellow residents. Lawrence's responses cannot be understood apart from the specific context from which they arose.

The response and recovery of the city are important factors related to the context. As we saw, the initial response of the city government was heralded, while the longer-term planning and recovery was disparaged for the most part. Quentin, who was documenting residents' positive stories of the flood, drew attention to this negative change in context:

> *I think the level of trust was very high immediately after, but again, due to the state of things today, some of that has been lost [...] if you go down on fourth street in Czech Village, there's a house sitting in the road. It's been sitting in the road since June 13th [...] the trust of being able to ask the government or your leaders to help and expect them to do something just isn't there right now [...] it trickles down to everybody. If you can't trust your leaders, who can you trust? It was great at first, but we've lost . . . we've lost whatever strides we made, and that's a shame.*

The current context affects how disastrous the flood was or is for each resident, especially the more vulnerable as their vulnerabilities are exploited. As a resident's current situation varies, so alters his or her perception of social capital after the flood.

It is tempting to write a tale of two cities in Cedar Rapids: one city comprised of residents that see social capital gains from the benchmark experience of the flood—a citizenry more resilient, united, and intent on improving their community; the other city of harder-hit residents, still rebuilding their homes and lives, that do not see how social capital in the community can profit from such a devastating experience.

However, these varying perspectives reflect neither discord nor disagreement. To be sure, the decimation of some neighborhoods, renewal of social rifts, disappointments with the city's recovery efforts, and the enormity of the event itself have disproportionately hurt a vulnerable minority of residents and sullied much of the collective feeling of "we are all in this together" that was, by nearly all accounts, evident early on. Nevertheless, variations in the residents' perceptions of social capital are more illustrative of their different focuses and current predicaments—and, by extension, their vulnerabilities and buoyancies—rather than a disavowal of all that was commonly shared and experienced in the Cedar Rapids flood of 2008.

Chapter Nine

Conclusion

My field research in Cedar Rapids demonstrates that natural disasters impact social capital in nuanced and complicated ways, based on human vulnerabilities and buoyancies.

At first glance, it seemed that residents perceived two different versions of Cedar Rapids in terms of social capital—one city with expanded social networks and bolstered civic norms moving forward together and another city "stuck" in the present where social networks had washed away with neighborhoods and disharmony swelled as tensions heightened. On further scrutiny, however, it was clear that respondents' perceptions of social capital were less contradictory than they first appeared. Changes in circumstances and disparities in conditions, rather than opposing world-views or irreconcilable opinions, influenced the residents' perspectives of social capital after the flood. With the advent of new problems over time, the condition of more vulnerable residents deteriorated, while more buoyant residents returned to relative normalcy. This in turn influenced whether a resident was preoccupied with the recovery or the response, whether they offered a positive or negative opinion of the city government and whether they expressed a positive or negative view of community life after the flood.

Four interrelated factors left residents alternatively more vulnerable or more buoyant: background characteristics, the structural and cultural aspects of social capital, and the current, contextually specific situation in Cedar Rapids. The loss of social networks, the collapse of the therapeutic community, and delays with the recovery were particularly damaging for the more vulnerable. The flood was always more disastrous for vulnerable residents than for buoyant ones; however, it become increasingly disastrous as problems mounted and they became even more vulnerable over time because they lacked the social networks and therapeutic community norms needed to cope and rebuild.

Although the therapeutic community cannot be artificially created and social networks cannot be easily rebuilt, the key elements of both can be stimulated or procured to help victims mitigate their loss and hasten their return to normalcy. More fortunate victims and unaffected individuals can resist the temptation to simply "move on with their lives and leave behind those still immersed in the experience" by offering their time, expertise, and social networks, in addition to any financial donations, to the hardest-hit residents (Kaniasty and Norris 1999, 47).

The government can help facilitate channels for communication and information sharing between residents to ensure that everyone's needs are known, if not fulfilled. Field researchers, interested in understanding the thoughts and experiences of different members of a studied population, can also play a role in this communication-promoting capacity by working with the government and civil society organizations to facilitate community forums for open dialogue and information sharing.

This case study explored a largely unexplored link between two well-developed fields in the context of a recent event. It is a work of first words, not last. Cedar Rapids is a relatively homogenous mid-sized city with low levels of poverty and without heavy social conflict. The city is not especially typical, though no city can be taken as a microcosm for wider society (Crow and Allan 1994, 196). The goal of this study was to understand, in nuanced terms, how a particular flood impacted an outlined version of social capital in a city through the perceptions of its residents. Reliability was neither sought nor attained (nor, indeed, possible).[1]

My field research offers a high-resolution snapshot rather than a comprehensive report on the flood. The organizational capacity of the city was only nominally covered; thus, a significant component of community life was skimmed over.[2] Many key groups were not included in the small sample, most notably young people and residents who left the area after the flood. The recovery is not over, and many residents agreed that post-traumatic stress and despair were just setting in after my first site visit: "We are only hitting the tip of the iceberg [in] acknowledging our own pain," said Alice.[3] Finally, the long-term impact of the flood on social capital won't be visible for many years. Ongoing contextual research is needed to obtain a more complete understanding of the June 2008 Flood in Cedar Rapids and its impact on community.

As this case study indicates, there is a distinct need for a research approach that captures nuance when studying social capital and disasters. As a field of inquiry, social capital would be well-served to reduce its reliance on the top-down approach of survey-measurement and opt instead for more bottom-up, contextual understandings rooted in qualitative community case studies (van Deth 2008, 160-161; Silverman 2001, 235; Dudwick et al. 2006).

By integrating the structural and cultural aspects and the public and private good notions of Putnam and Bourdieu in the Commons analogy, we reached a pragmatic understanding of social capital as a highly stratified and differentiated collective good—an underutilized framework for understanding and assessing social capital that, when applied, can discern resource advantages and disadvantages in access, use, and power between individuals and within communities. To put it slightly differently, a flexible framework that can discern the buoyancies and vulnerabilities that sustain residents or leave them "stuck" long after the floodwaters recede.

As we observed, social capital fluctuates in complex ways after a disaster, based on a combination of vulnerabilities and buoyancies. The study of social capital and disaster demands a research scheme mindful of "the complicated, ever-evolving, and often conflicted feelings within individual[s]," able to capture extensive nuance, elusive detail, and curious fluctuation (Sokolove 2008). Social capital as a field of inquiry would be well-served if researchers reduced their reliance on the top-down approach of survey measurement and opted instead for more bottom-up, contextual understandings rooted in qualitative community case studies (van Deth 2008).

Disaster studies must be incorporated into future social capital research, and vice versa, narrowing the curious gap between canons. The overlap is apparent: both fields seek to understand community functionality and identify inequalities within complex social systems. The study of social capital is a study of structural and cultural resource advantages between individuals and within societies. The study of disasters is a study of human and societal vulnerabilities as exposed by natural hazards. A more interdisciplinary future between both fields stands to offer each key insight into its own fundamental concerns. As this book illustrates, the need to synthesize disaster studies and social capital is conspicuous; together, they provide an excellent opportunity to study normally latent social processes that help us understand the structural and cultural order of a community.

Appendix 1

Research Design

Natural disasters occur all the time, all over the world. Why study a non-fatal flood in Cedar Rapids, Iowa? I made the selection based on five compelling reasons—a mixture of pragmatism, personal interest, and attributes of the case.

1. *"Prototypical."* The Cedar Rapids flood was fairly "prototypical." It was generally a case of human vulnerabilities being exploited by natural hazards, rather than human-induced hazards. Although there is no such thing as a prototypical flood, there are occasions when unusual or severe circumstances make an event less natural or more disastrous (Erikson 1979). In this case, the flood was almost unanimously recognized as a natural event by respondents.
2. *Access.* With close family members living twenty minutes from Cedar Rapids, I was fortunate to have a degree of privileged access to the area. My aunt is a well-connected professor who put me in touch with a number of college staff members and community members that became key informants and gatekeepers. Also, use of their car proved essential to this study, as I navigated around the city to conduct thirty interviews over the course of two site visits.

3. *Familiarity.* Because of my family connections in the area, I have visited before. I am comfortable in Cedar Rapids and its environs. I was not immediately perceived as an outsider given my familiar American accent, mannerisms, and appearance (cf. Naples 1996).

4. *Size.* I found both disaster and city manageable: not too big, but certainly big enough. With a population of about 125,000 people, Cedar Rapids is a mid-sized Midwestern city that is easily traversable by car, with developed organizational capacity, diverse industries, and an array of different types of people and neighborhoods. It experienced a disaster that was devastating but not incapacitating in destruction. The flood was historic for the area, but would not be a particular anomaly by wider comparison.

5. *Timeliness.* Just over 100 days had passed since the flood occurred when I first arrived in Cedar Rapids. I was concerned that even this relatively brief interlude would make the disaster less relevant. On the contrary, the flood was still at the forefront of discourse in Cedar Rapids. The city's newspaper, *The Gazette*, featured flood-related stories on the front page every day of my fieldwork. The flood was "*the* topic of conversation*" among residents, said Gloria, a flood-displaced renter from the Taylor School area.

Semi-structured qualitative interviews were the appropriate choice of methods. This exploratory study sought to understand "the complicated, ever-evolving and often conflicted feelings within individual[s]" (Sokolove 2008). Therefore, it demanded a nuanced understanding of social capital access and use. Personal interviews allowed me to go in-depth in context and look at the local dimension of social capital in a way that large-scale surveys neglect, a common oversight of social capital research today (Dudwick et al. 2006; van Deth 2008, 160-161).

Sample. Interviewees were selected based on the recommendations of gatekeepers and key informants, as well as my own personal, often random social encounters. Only a few control variables were used in selecting respondents: age and gender, comparable damage sustained in the flood, and length of time in the area. My first site visit extended 11 days in Cedar Rapids. I conducted 30 interviews between 45 and 90 minutes. 14 were victim interviews, 14 were key informant and gatekeeper interviews, and 2 were pilot interviews. In my second site visit, four years later, I reengaged with half of the flood victims and key informants from my first site visit.

"Flood victim" and "key informant" were the two imperfect conceptual categories used to classify interviewees. The primary distinction between these categories was the reason why they were chosen to be interviewed. Victims were residents of Cedar Rapids whose personal residence or place of work was damaged by the flood. The value-laden term "victim" is not meant to prejudge, although it is cumbersome (Bolin et al. 1998, 27). It should be noted that many flood victims saw themselves as *survivors* or merely *people affected by the flood*. Informants were locals mostly from Cedar Rapids (although one or two came from the suburb of Marion) who were involved in the flood recovery or were knowledgeable about the community. The categories are not mutually exclusive: some informants' workplaces and dwellings were damaged, and some victims knew the community very well.

Nevertheless, some general substantive differences do appear between flood victims and informants that make such a distinction necessary beyond the ease of categorization. For instance, over 90% of victims whose personal residences were damaged were still rebuilding four months after the flood. These individuals were displaced, staying with family, short-term lodgings, FEMA trailers, or, in one case, a tent. By contrast, only 14% of key informants sustained any damage from the flood.

A convenience sample was used. Though clearly not meant for fair representation or randomness (Ursano et al. 1994, 15), the snowball method was adequate as a random sample was not possible. I lacked full knowledge of my population and would have undermined randomness by inadvertently omitting key groups, such as people who moved out of the area. My foremost interest was in access and detail. My goal was to gain a deeper understanding of my case study in order to facilitate the development of an analytic framework and new explanatory concepts, a procedure which Glaser and Strauss (1967) refer to as theoretical sampling.

Interviews. The semi-structured approach used in this study required narration and order: and chances for elaboration by the interviewee, but guiding control by the interviewer. Answers flowed in a free-form fashion, interposed with probing questions to progress the interview forward as necessary (Cisin and Clark 1962, 27). This flexible interview approach enabled discovery and allowed disaster victims leeway in describing experiences in their own words (Fielding & Thomas 2008, 124 & 247). An interview guide was used to provide topical structure and guide these purposeful conversations (Simmons 2008, 186). In order to test the ordering of questions and the cultural-appropriateness of the interview's style, two pilot interviews were conducted with local contacts.

Initially in my interviews, I planned to avoid direct mention of the flood to see whether an interviewee independently (i.e. unprimed) brought up the flood when discussing current civic behaviors and social relations. This was meant to be a simple way to gauge the impression the flood did or did not make on a respondent. But this proved very impractical.

First, interviewees assumed that I was uninformed or playing games. I was received curiously and less-than-seriously. For instance, when asked "Can you think of anything that has happened here in the last year that has either improved or weakened the feeling of togetherness in this community?" interviewees would look at me expectantly or nervously chuckle, as if I should add "*besides* the flood?" Many respondents added this obvious remark to the question themselves.

Second, each of the four ways I accessed "victims" required mention of the flood: unplanned face-to-face encounters, "cold-calling" via email, gatekeeper-led introductions, or gatekeeper-facilitated interactions (gatekeeper gives contact details but does not personally introduce). For the former two, disclosure of the specific reason for requesting an interview was necessary. In regards to the latter two, I had no control over what gatekeepers told respondents, but I assume that my focus on the flood was offered as an explanation for why I wanted to interview them.

My apprehension of the *no mention of the flood* approach was corroborated about twenty minutes into my first interview. After I gained the trust of this particularly skeptical interviewee, he revealed that he had lied about when he planned to return to his residence and had taken pictures of me walking by his house. After this episode, full disclosure of my research topic was given. The switch made me more relaxed and offered a fuller informed consent.

I first introduced myself to potential interviewees as a graduate student who wanted to learn about the flood as part of my thesis. I sought to gain a respondent's trust by offering enough personal background information without seeming overly foreign. I believe most flood victims thought I was from Iowa, a helpful assumption I did not proactively dispel. To "provide a framework of trust," I followed the guidance of Lee (1993, 98) and conducted interviews with a non-condemnatory attitude and reassurances of privacy and confidentiality. Interviews were characterized by a high degree of positive interaction and high levels of cooperation.

Brief extemporaneous notes were taken while a voice recorder captured the interview for later review (Creswell 2003, 186). There were a few occasions when a voice recorder was not used in order to ensure an interviewee's comfort.

Ethics. Ethics were appropriately considered in the design and implementation of this study. The chief ethical concern was the potential harm caused to respondents by discussing a sensitive, potentially traumatic subject (Sapsford and Abbott 1996, 320). This concern proved nearly irrelevant, as residents were accustomed to discussing the flood four months on, and certainly four years later when I returned for another site visit. Respondents who appeared emotionally or financially unstable were referred to local support services.

Categories. Each interview was divided into five categories:

1. *Social capital in general;*
2. *Damage and relative devastation from the flood;*
3. *Flood responses and recovery;*
4. *Social capital in relation to the flood; and*
5. *Background characteristics (control variables).*

In category 2, respondents discussed their personal experiences of the flood. In category 3, respondents discussed how the government, news media, and wider community were perceived after the flood, including long-term planning and rebuilding efforts. In category 5, relevant background information was gathered, including standard social capital controls (e.g. education, socio-economic status, and longevity in the area) and variables that uniquely confound the impact of a natural disaster on social capital (e.g. home ownership).

Categories 1 and 4, which are the focus of this manuscript, evaluate social capital contextually through its structural and cultural components. Subcategories focused on:

1. Social capital as more of a private good with resource stratification and differentiation, assessed by *access and power* (in-

tegration, exclusion and relative hardship), *bonds with friends*, and *barriers to connecting*;

2. Social capital as more of a collective good with societal advantages and disadvantages, assessed by *norms of trustworthiness* and *sense of solidarity*; and
3. Social capital as mixed (roughly), assessed by *norms* (reciprocity, helpfulness, and appropriate crisis-situation behaviors), *sources of support* (family, friends, neighbors, and community), and *remembrances* (memories, representations, and reflections).

One important note: this study does not measure *actual* fluctuations of social capital. Such a feat is unachievable here. Precise time-scaled longitudinal data would be required from before and after the disaster. Controls for convoluting factors (length of residency, severity of impact, size and quality of social network) would need to be tested and in place. Rather than try to measure what is inaccessible, *I chose* to evaluate *perceptions* of social capital by focusing on each interviewee's subjective thoughts and experiences.

Data Collection Biases. Reflexivity affected my interviews on many fronts, including through background disparities between my respondents and me (Hammersley and Atkinson 2000, 18). Aside from obvious discrepancies—I am not from the area; I did not endure the flood—I was substantially younger and had more years of formal education than most respondents. Power dynamics were surely in play.

The selection bias occurred in two important senses. First, gatekeepers and key informants referred me to some types of residents over others. When I asked a gatekeeper to put me in touch with residents affected by the flood, I assume they contacted *friends and co-workers* from their social networks with roughly the same socioeconomic status who would be *willing* to speak about their *particularly bad* flood experiences. I doubt gatekeepers thought to send me to friends who were in emotional or psychological tatters or who were only mildly affected by the flood. Much of my sample was gathered by gatekeepers' at their own discretion, on which I can only speculate.

Second, all of my interviewees live in or nearby Cedar Rapids. Some townspeople, likely those worst hit by the flood, have already left. This is important: I did not interview anyone who had left the area. My sample is skewed towards residents who decided to stay in Cedar Rapids, which overlooks the crucial (but nearly impossible to locate) subset of community members who left the community. As Lawrence put it during my return visit four years later, "the people who were hurt the worst . . . they disappeared. You don't hear from them anymore. Many of these people had little houses worth $60,000 dollars. They were disposable people. Their houses were gone, and so were they . . . they became a non-entity. They were no longer valued at all."

In my first site visit, I spent 11 days in Cedar Rapids, capturing 17 hours of recordings and more than 100 pages of notes from about 30 different flood victims and key informants. The qualitative analysis used in this project was a limited version of grounded theory. Unfamiliar relationships and generated theories were explored rather than predetermined hypotheses (Strauss and Corbin 1998, 13). To generate theories, the researcher "flip-flopped" between data and ideas, research experience and concepts. This type of inductive approach, used in prominent social capital qualitative method guides (Dudwick et al. 2006), led to the development of analytical frames and the emergence of more concepts (Boulton and Hammersley 1996, 280; Pidgeon 1996, 82). Time and resource limitations prevented me from embracing other desirable aspects of grounded theory—most notably, only two site visits and no constant comparative method (Creswell 1998, 56 and 98).

After two or three interviews, repeated issues were assigned conceptual labels (*codes*) to "identify themes, patterns, processes and relationships" (Lofland and Lofland 1995, 186). When I returned to Cambridge, I continued this process of conceptual development, coding, and thematic analysis with a bit more rigor, roughly following Fielding's four steps of qualitative coding (2008, 336): read data and search for significance; reread data and search for patterns and anomalies; interpret data, make category titles and codes; and develop hypotheses about repeating patterns, gather best examples of types, and strong verbatim responses.

All interview notes and other materials were amassed and reviewed. In coding and analysis, I relied on interview notes, significant concepts, quotes from recordings, and my personal notepad, which I wrote in every evening during my fieldwork. It consisted of notes on everyday people and events, data collection procedures, preliminary analysis, and sequence of interviews (Lofland and Lofland 1995). The identities of all interviewees were replaced by aliases, so as to ensure confidentiality.

After reviewing these materials, I created a one to two page document for each interviewee that was divided into *basic information and damage*, *responses and recovery*, and *social capital*. After standardizing my interviews, I reread all documents to search for significant phrases and ideas, with the aim of being "sensitized" to the properties and dimensions of the data so as to allow concepts to "emerge from the data" (Strauss and Corbin 1998, 33 and 59).

I then looked for topics and issues in the text through open coding, assembling a mixture of descriptive and explanatory codes. At this stage the coding list was detailed and specific, with numerous entries and without clear direction (Hodkinson 2008, 87). It was winnowed down next.

Once compiled, codes were synthesized through axial coding, a process that involves searching for patterns, relationships, and repetitions between codes. Two themes emerged: *unity* and *change*. Each theme was found to elicit the contrasts between different interviewees and the conflicts within a single respondent's perspective. These variations formed the basis for the analysis of how the Cedar Rapids flood impacted social capital (Fielding 2008, 325).

In open-ended interviews, respondents are not confined to choose an answer from a limited number of prescribed choices. Therefore, a more interpretative validity is sought (Altheide and Johnson 1998, 286).

I believe that my decision to interview both flood victims and key informants helped me reach a greater degree of interpretative validity. Different members of a community have different levels of access to and use of community resources, despite the fact that all members are theoretically equal (as discussed earlier in my Commons analogy). "Victims" and "informants" come from different vantage points both pre- and post-disaster: on the whole, the flood victims I spoke with wielded less influence, held positions of less power, and were more likely to be directly and adversely affected by the flood. When the subjective accounts of both types of respondent were aggregated, I obtained a nuance-rich portrait of events related to the flood. Moreover, recurring concepts and themes emerged when the stories of my respondents were pooled, through which I obtained a degree of interpretative validity.

Although a majority of the data gathered in this project is retrospective, the typical problems associated with the recall bias are nullified, such as determining whether information is valid (Wilson 1996, 107; Johnson, Feinberg, and Johnston 1994, 180). I *wanted* respondents to give their subjective perceptions of social capital before and after the flood, infused with their present perspectives (Bergman & Magnusson 1990, 23). Standard concerns with retrospective data were muted.

The fallacy of aggregation is built-in to this project (Frankfort-Nachmias & Nachmias 1996, 55). This problem encumbers many studies of social capital and arises from a quandary that has not been fully answered yet: how to draw inferences about groups and communities whilst gathering evidence from individuals.[1] I cannot solve this problem here, but I can avoid most of the fallacy's distortive effects by drawing out widely-held trends and themes from the nuanced accounts of my thirty respondents.

Appendix 2

Maps

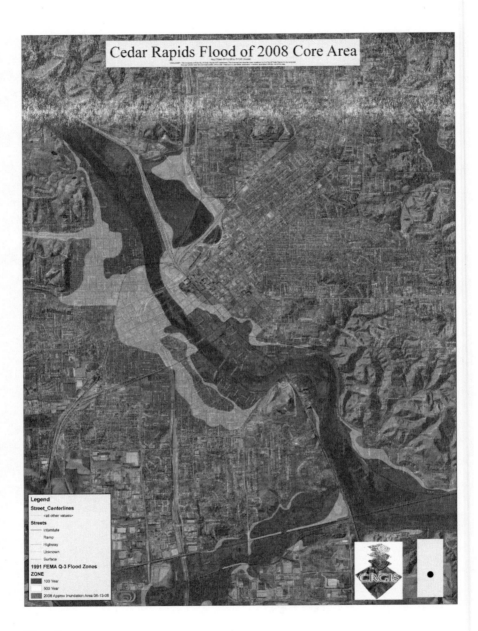

Cedar Rapids Flood of 2008 Core Area

Map 1.

Map 2.

Notes

1. INTRODUCTION

1. I avoid most use of the contentious term *natural disasters* until I can explain the problems associated with its standard usage in Chapter 2. The focus of this book *is* natural disasters, but slapdash use of the term before it is adequately conceptualized would be more hindrance than help for my arguments.

2. Social capital is minimally defined here as it is greatly elaborated upon in Chapter 3.

3. The names of residents have been changed in this book to protect their identities.

2. NATURAL DISASTERS

1. Natural hazards include earthquakes, floods, hurricanes, tornadoes, volcanoes, and tsunamis (Fischer 1998, 5).

3. SOCIAL CAPITAL

1. Hooghe and Stolle (2003, 1) begin their book by stating "Less than five years ago, a book like this would have started with an elaborate definition of the concept of social capital. Today, this no longer seems necessary." Five years later, in a telling dose of irony, Stolle and Hooghe each contribute chapters to *The Handbook of Social Capital* (2008), a tome in which the first 195 pages are dedicated to still-contested "Conceptual Issues" in the social capital debate.

2. I argue for a basic framework that identifies the essential features of social capital, not a rigid definition. The latter is impractical and would stifle empirical creativity and application, whereas a practical framework would enhance the field by improving communicability, comparability, and detail (Castiglione 2008, 20).

3. James Coleman is a leading voice in the social capital debate as well, but I have opted to concentrate on a very specific set of similarities and divergences between Putnam and Bourdieu that will provide the contrast and flexibility in conceptualization that is needed to analyze social capital through primary interviews in the context of a natural disaster. The definitions I offer are fundamental to each scholar's broader conceptualization, but by no means should they be taken as indicative of the totality of their theories on the topic. For instance, Putnam is renowned for positively connecting social capital levels to the functioning of democratic systems, a discussion I minimize in this text.

4. Bourdieu (1986) expands on the structural aspects on page 243 (social capital as "connections") and the cultural aspects on page 256 (social capital includes "manners").

5. See Foley, Edwards, & Diani 2001, 276.

4. AN ANALOGY

1. Technically speaking, Commons are *owned* by one person or entity, not by everybody, and *made available* for public access and use. My analogy is directed towards a few *specified* social functions of an extremely sociable Commons, rather than fullness in the comparison. I offer the analogy at its face value.

2. This does not refer to the finite resources of the Commons itself that would limit the number of users or extent of access. I assume these resources are unlimited (i.e. no *Tragedy of the Commons*).

3. It should be noted that "negative" social behavior like ostracism is neither inherently negative nor devoid of social capital. Quite the contrary to both: regarding the former, social boundaries can serve important purposes in social systems in maintaining law and order, reinforcing acceptable behavior, and setting community guidelines. In regards to the latter, social ostracism demands social capital, as it is an example of a set of rigid norms of an in-group being threatened or rejected (in reality or not). Social capital can support nefarious purposes (not "squealing" in organized crime groups) and cause a leveling-down of behavior (if lazy workers are a majority in a worksite, the expectations for all will lower).

5. THE FLOOD

1. Williams, Zinner, and Ellis (1999, 7) discuss the important role of local authorities in disaster recovery.

2. Imam is an Arabic word that means leader and is used to describe the leader of a mosque.

6. THE COMMUNITY

1. See Echterling and Wylie (1999, 340) for a discussion of the blurring of distinction between disaster helpers and victims.

2. Block by Block was created in 2009 (after my initial interviews were conducted) to counteract this type of uncertainty and incentive misalignment between neighbors. The service project used an effective and much heralded "one block at a time" approach to provide rebuilding assistance to 25 blocks and 278 homes. The partnership implementing the program ended in 2012.

9. CONCLUSION

1. For discussion of the dubiousness of reliability in qualitative studies, see Crow and Allan (1994, 195) and Golafshani (2003).

2. For discussion of the "organized disorganization" of organizations in disaster response, see Fischer (1998, 89-90). For a critical assessment of the role existing institutions often play during disaster (in contrast to the emergent, improvisational role of civil society), see Solnit (2009, 127).

3. For discussion of trauma and its impact on disaster-affected communities, see Kaniasty and Norris (1999, 40); Erikson (1995, 186 and 242); Kalayjian (1999, 99); and Dynes (1970, 96). For the role of social capital in minimizing risk of PTSD in Iowa after a 1993 flood, see Ollenburger and Tobin (1998).

APPENDIX 1. RESEARCH DESIGN

1. Scholars who follow Putnam tend to ask about formal group participation to gauge social capital. This approach is widely criticized as outdated in today's cosmopolitan-networked society (Arneil 2006, 227; Boggs 2002, 186).

References

Aldrich, D. P. (2012). *Building Resilience: Social Capital in Post-Disaster Recovery.* Chicago: University of Chicago Press.

Alexander, D. (1993). *Natural Disasters.* London: UCL Press.

Altheide, D. L. and Johnson, J. M. (1998). "Criteria for Assessing Interpretive Validity in Qualitative Research," in Denzin, N. K., and Lincoln, Y. S. (eds.). *Collecting and Interpreting Qualitative Materials* London: Sage, pp. 283–312.

Arneil, B. (2006). *Diverse Communities: the Problem with Social Capital.* Cambridge: Cambridge University Press.

Arrow, K. (2000). "Observations on Social Capital." *Social Capital: A Multifaceted Perspective.* Washington, DC: The World Bank.

Barnshaw, J., and Trainor, J. (2007). "Race, Class, and Capital amidst the Hurricane Katrina Diaspora," in Brunsma, D. L., Overfelt, D., and Picou, J. S. (eds.). *The Sociology of Katrina.* Lanham, MD: Rowman and Littlefield, pp. 91–105.

Barton, A. H. (1969). *Communities in Disaster: A Sociological Analysis of Collective Stress Situations.* Garden City, New York: Doubleday.

Bergman, L. R. and Magnusson, D. (1990). "General Issues About Data Quality in Longitudinal Research," in Magnusson and Bergman (eds.). *Data Quality in Longitudinal Research.* Cambridge: Cambridge University Press.

Blaikie, P., Cannon, T., Davis, I., and Wisner, B. (1994). *At Risk: Natural Hazards, People's Vulnerability and Disasters.* Routledge: New York.

Boggs, C. (2002). "Social Capital as Political Fantasy," in McLean, Schultz, D. A., and Steger, M. B. (eds.). *Social Capital: Critical Perspectives on Community and Bowling Alone.* New York: NYU Press, pp. 183–200.

Bolin, R., Jackson, M., and Crist, A. (1998). "Gender Inequality, Vulnerability, and Disaster: Issues in Theory and Research," in Enarson and Morrow (eds.). *The Gendered Terrain of Disaster: Through Women's Eyes.* London: Praeger, pp. 27–44.

Boulton, D. and Hammersley, M. (1996). "Analysis of Unstructured Data," in Sapsford, R. and Jupp, V. (eds,). *Data Collection and Analysis.* London: Sage, pp. 282–297.

Bourdieu, P. (1986). "The Forms of Capital," in Richardson, J. (ed.). *The Handbook for Theory and Research for the Sociology of Education.* Westport, Connecticut: Greenwood Press, pp. 241–258.

Bourdieu, P., and Wacquant, L. (1992). *An Invitation to Reflexive Sociology.* Chicago and London: University of Chicago Press.

Carr, L. J. (1932). "Disaster and the Sequence-Pattern Concept of Change." *American Journal of Sociology.* Vol. 38 (2), pp. 207–218.

Castiglione, D., van Deth, J. W., and Wolleb, G. (2008). "Social Capital's Fortune: An Introduction," in Castiglione, van Deth, and Wolleb (eds.). *The Handbook of Social Capital.* Oxford: Oxford University Press, pp. 1–10.

Castiglione, D. (2008). "Social Capital as a Research Programme," in Castiglione, van Deth, J. W., and Wolleb, G. (eds.). *The Handbook of Social Capital.* Oxford: Oxford University Press, pp. 15–21.

Cisin, I. H., and Clark, W. B. (1962). "The Methodological Challenge of Disaster Research," in Baker, G. W., and Chapman, D. W. (eds.). *Man and Society in Disaster.* New York: Basic Books, pp. 23–49.

Clarke, L. B. (2006). *Worst Cases: Terror and Catastrophe in the Popular Imagination.* Chicago: University of Chicago Press.

Creswell, J. W. (2003). *Research Design: Qualitative, Quantitative, and Mixed Methods Approaches.* London: Sage.

Crow, G., and Allan, G. (1994). *Community Life: An Introduction to Local Social Relations.* New York and London: Harvester Wheatsheaf.

Dombrowsky, W. R. (1998). "Again and Again—Is a Disaster What We Call a 'Disaster,'" in Quarantelli, E. L. (ed.). *What Is A Disaster? Perspectives on the Question.* London: Routledge, pp. 19–30.

Drabek, T. E. (1986). *Human System Responses to Disaster: An Inventory of Sociological Findings.* New York: Springer-Verlag.

Dudwick, N., Kuehnast, K., Nyhan Jones, V., and Woolcock, M. (2006). "Analyzing Social Capital in Context: A Guide to Using Qualitative Methods and Data." *World Bank Institute.* Available online at http://siteresources.world bank.org/WBI/ Resources/Analyzing_Social_Capital_in_Context-FINAL.pdf.

Dynes, R. (1970). *Organized Behavior in Disaster.* Lexington, Mass.: Heath Lexington Books.

Dynes, R. (2002). "The Importance of Social Capital in Disaster Response." Preliminary Paper #327. University of Delaware Disaster Research Center.

Echterling, L. G., and Wylie, M. L. (1999). "In the Public Arena: Disaster as a Socially Constructed Problem," in Gist, R., and Lubin, B. (eds.). *Response to Disaster: Psychosocial, Community, and Ecological Approaches.* Philadelphia and London: Brunner/Mazel, pp. 327–346.

Erikson, Kai T. (1979). *In the Wake of the Flood.* London: Allen & Unwin.

Erikson, K. (1994). *A New Species of Trouble: Explorations in Disaster, Trauma, and Community.* New York and London: Norton.

Field, J. (2008). *Social Capital* (2nd edition). London: Routledge.

Fielding, J. (2008). "Coding and Managing Data," in Gilbert, N. (ed.). *Researching Social Life* (3rd edition). London: Sage, pp. 323–352.

Fielding, N., and Thomas, H. (2008). "Qualitative Interviewing," in Gilbert, N. (ed.). *Researching Social Life* (3rd edition). London: Sage, pp. 245–265.

Fine, B. (2001). "It Ain't Social and It Ain't Capital," in Morrow, V. (ed.). *An Appropriate Capital-isation?: Questioning Social Capital.* London: London School of Economics, Gender Institute, pp. 11–15.

Fischer, H. W. (1998). *Response to Disaster: Fact Versus Fiction & Its Perpetuation: The Sociology of Disaster.* Lanham, MD, and Oxford: University Press of America.

Foley, M. W., Edwards, B., and Diani, M. (2001). "Social Capital Reconsidered," in Edwards, Foley, and Diani (eds.). *Beyond Tocqueville: Civil Society and the Social Capital Debate in Comparative Perspective.* Hanover, NH, and London: University Press of New England, pp. 266–80.

Fothergill, A. (1998). "The Neglect of Gender in Disaster Work: An Overview of the Literature," in Enarson and Morrow (eds.). *The Gendered Terrain of Disaster: Through Women's Eyes.* London: Praeger, pp. 11–25.

Frankfort-Nachmias, C., and Nachmias, D. (1996). *Research Methods in the Social Sciences.* London: St. Martin's Press.

Fritz, C. E. (1961). "Disaster," in Merton, R. K., and Nisbet, R. A. (eds.). *Contemporary Social Problems.* New York: Harcourt, Brace & World, pp. 651–694.

Glaser, B. G. and Strauss, A. L. (1967). *The Discovery of Grounded Theory: Strategies for Qualitative Research.* London: Weidenfeld and Nicholson.

Goddard, R. D. (2003). "Relational Networks, Social Trust, and Norms: A Social Capital Perspective on Students' Chances of Academic Success." *Educational Evaluation and Policy Analysis*, Vol. 25, No. 1, pp. 59–74.

Golafshani, N. (2003). "Understanding Reliability and Validity in Qualitative Research." *The Qualitative Report.* Vol. 8 (4): pp. 597–607.

Halpern, D. (2005). *Social Capital.* Cambridge: Polity Press.

Harriss, J. (2001). "Social Capital Construction and the Consolidation of Civil Society," Development Studies Institute, Working Paper No. 01–16, London School of Economics.

Hodkinson, P. (2008). "Grounded Theory and Inductive Research," Gilbert, N. (ed.). *Researching Social Life* (3rd edition). London: Sage, pp. 80–100.

Hooghe, M., and Stolle, D. (2003). "Introduction: Generating Social Capital," in Hooghe and Stolle (eds.). *Generating Social Capital: Civil Society and Institutions in Comparative Perspective.* New York: Palgrave Macmillan, pp. 1–18.

Hooghe, M. (2008). "Voluntary Associations and Socialization," in Castiglione, D., van Deth, J.W., and Wolleb, G. [eds.]. *The Handbook of Social Capital.* Oxford: Oxford University Press, pp. 568–593.

Horvat, E., McNamara, Weininger, E. B. and Lareau, A. (2003). "From Social Ties to Social Capital: Class Differences in the Relations between Schools and

Parent Networks." *American Educational Research Journal*, Vol. 40, No. 2, pp. 319–351.

Johnson, N. R., Feinberg, W. E., and Johnston, D. M. (1994). "Microstructure and Panic: The Impact of Social Bonds on Individual Action in Collective Flight from the Beverly Hills Supper Club Fire," in Dynes, R., and Tierney, K. (eds.). *Disasters, Collective Behavior, and Social Organization.* Newark: University of Delaware Press, pp. 168–189.

Kalayjian, A. (1999). "Coping Through Meaning: The Community Response to the Earthquake in Armenia," in Zinner, E. S., and Williams, M. B. (eds). *When a Community Weeps: Case Studies in Group Survivorship.* Philadelphia and London: Brunner/Mazel, pp. 87–101.

Kaniasty, K., and Norris, F. (1995). "In Search of Altruistic Community: Patterns of Social Support Mobilization Following Hurricane Hugo." *American Journal of Community Psychology*, Vol. 23(4), pp. 447–77.

Kaniasty, K., and Norris, F. (1999). "The Experience of Disaster: Individuals and Communities Sharing Trauma," in Gist, R., and Lubin, B. (eds.). *Response to Disaster: Psychosocial, Community, and Ecological Approaches.* Philadelphia and London: Brunner/Mazel, pp. 25–61.

Kawachi, I., and Berkman, L. F. (eds.) (2000). *Social Epidemiology.* Oxford: Oxford University Press, pp. 174–190.

Klinenberg, Eric. (1994). *Heat Wave: A Social Autopsy of Disaster in Chicago.* Chicago: University of Chicago.

Lee, D. (1993*). Man-Made Catastrophes: from the Burning of Rome to the Lockerbie Crash.* New York: Facts on File.

Lee, R. M. (1993). *Doing Research on Sensitive Topics.* London: Sage.

Lin, N. (2001). *Social Capital: A Theory of Social Structure and Action.* Cambridge: Cambridge University Press.

Lofland, J. and Lofland, L. (1995). *Analyzing Social Settings: A Guide to Qualitative Observation and Analysis.* Belmont, CA: Wadsworth.

McLean, S. L., Schultz, D. A., and Steger, M. B. (2002). "Introduction," in McLean, Schultz, and Steger (eds.). *Social Capital: Critical Perspectives on Community and Bowling Alone.* New York: NYU Press, pp. 1–17.

MCEER Information Service. (2008). "Iowa—Midwest Flood News & Statistics." State University of New York at Buffalo. Viewed on 28 November 2008 at http://mceer.buffalo.edu/infoservice/disasters/iowa-flood-news-statistics .asp.

Nakagawa, Y. and Shaw, R. (2004). "Social Capital: A Missing Link to Disaster Recovery." *International Journal of Mass Emergencies and Disasters.* Vol. 22 (1), pp. 5–34.

Naples, N. A. (1996). "A Feminist Revisiting of the Insider/Outsider Debate: The 'Outsider Phenomenon' in Rural Iowa." *Qualitative Sociology*, Vol. 19, pp. 83–106.

Norris, F. H., Phifer, J. F., and Kaniasty, K. (1994). "Individual and Community Reactions to the Kentucky Floods: Findings from a Longitudinal Study of Older Adults," in Ursano, McCaughey and Fullerton (eds.). *Individual and*

Community Responses to Trauma and Disaster: The Structure of Human Chaos. Cambridge: Cambridge University Press, pp. 378–400.

Ollenburger, J. C., and Tobin, G. A. (1998). "Women and Postdisaster Stress," in Enarson and Morrow (eds.). *The Gendered Terrain of Disaster: Through Women's Eyes.* London: Praeger, pp. 95–107.

Pelling, M. (2003). *The Vulnerability of Cities: Natural Disasters and Social Resilience.* London: Earthscan.

Picou, J. S., and Marshall, B. K. (2007). "Introduction: Katrina as Paradigm Shift: Reflections on Disaster Research in the Twenty-First Century," in Brunsma, D. L., Overfelt, D., and Picou (eds.). *The Sociology of Katrina.* Lanham, MD: Rowman and Littlefield, pp. 1–20.

Pidgeon, N. (1996). "Grounded theory: theoretical background," in Richardson, J. (ed.). *Handbook of Qualitative Research Methods for Psychology and the Social Sciences.* Derby, U.K.: BPS Books, pp. 75–85.

Portes, A. (1998). "Social Capital: Its Origins and Applications in Modern Sociology." *Annual Review of Sociology.* Vol. 24, pp. 1–24.

Putnam, R. D. (2000). *Bowling Alone: The Collapse and Revival of American Community.* New York: Simon & Schuster.

Putnam, R. D. (1993). *Making Democracy Work: Civic Traditions in Modern Italy.* New Jersey: Princeton University Press.

Quarantelli, E. L. (1985). "What is Disaster? The Need for Clarification in Definition and Conceptualization in Research," in Sowder, B. J. (ed.). *Disasters and Mental Health: Selected Contemporary Perspectives.* Rockville, MD: National Institute of Mental Health—Center for Mental Health Studies of Emergencies, pp. 41–73.

Quarantelli, E. L. (1987). "What Should We Study? Questions and Suggestions for Researchers About the Concept of Disasters." *International Journal of Mass Emergencies and Disasters.* Vol. 5 (1) (March 1987), pp. 9–15.

Quarantelli, E. L. (1998). *What Is A Disaster? Perspectives on the Question.* London: Routledge.

Quarantelli, E. L., and Dynes, R. R. (1985). "Community Responses to Disasters," in Sowder, B. J. (ed.). *Disasters and Mental Health: Selected Contemporary Perspectives.* Rockville, MD: National Institute of Mental Health—Center for Mental Health Studies of Emergencies, pp. 158–168.

Rozario, K. (2007). *The Culture of Calamity: Disaster and the Making of Modern America.* Chicago: University of Chicago Press.

Sapsford, R. and Abbott, P. (1996). "Ethics, Politics and Research," in Sapsford, R. and Jupp, V. (eds.). *Data Collection and Analysis.* London: Sage, pp. 317–342.

Simmons, R. (2008). "Questionnaires," in Gilbert, N. (ed.). *Researching Social Life* (3rd edition). London: Sage, pp. 182–205.

Silverman, D. (2001). *Interpreting Qualitative Data: Methods for Analyzing Talk, Text and Interaction.* London: Sage.

Smith, R. (2008). "Minorities, poor hit hard by flood." *The Gazette.* 13 August, pp. 1B and 6B.

Sokolove, M. (2008). "The Transformation." *The New York Times.* Page WK1 (New York edition).9 November 2009.

Solnit, R. (2009). *A Paradise Built in Hell: The Extraordinary Communities That Arise in Disaster.* New York: Penguin/Viking.

Sorokin, P. (1942). *Man and Society in Calamity: The Effects of War, Revolution, Famine, Pestilence upon Human Mind, Behavior, Social Organization, and Cultural Life.* New York: Dutton.

Strauss, A., and Corbin, J. (1998). *Basics of Qualitative Research: Techniques and Procedures for Developing Grounded Theory.* London: Sage.

Therborn, G. (2002). "Back to Norms! On the Scope and Dynamics of Norms and Normative Action." *Current Sociology.* Vol. 50 (6), pp. 863–880.

Tufty, B. (1978). *1001 Questions Answered about Earthquakes, Avalanches, Floods and Other Natural Disasters.* New York: Dover Publications.

Ursano, R. J., Fullerton, C. S., and McCaughey, B. G. (1994). "Trauma and Disaster," in Ursano, McCaughey and Fullerton (eds.). *Individual and Community Responses to Trauma and Disaster: The Structure of Human Chaos.* Cambridge: Cambridge University Press, pp. 3–27.

Uslaner, E. M. (2004). "Trust and Social Bonds: Faith in Others and Policy Outcomes Reconsidered." *Political Research Quarterly.* Volume 57, Number 3: 501–507.

van Deth, J. W. (2008). "Measuring Social Capital," in Castiglione, D., van Deth, and Wolleb, G. (eds.). *The Handbook of Social Capital.* Oxford: Oxford University Press, pp. 150–176.

Warren, M. E. (2008). "The Nature and Logic of Bad Social Capital," in Castiglione, D., van Deth, J. W., and Wolleb, G. (eds.). *The Handbook of Social Capital.* Oxford: Oxford University Press, pp. 122–149.

Wenger, D. E., and James, T. F. (1994). "The Convergence of Volunteers in a Consensus Crisis: The Case of the 1985 Mexico City Earthquake," in Dynes, R., and Tierney, K. (eds.). *Disasters, Collective Behavior, and Social Organization.* Newark: University of Delaware Press, pp. 229–243.

Williams, M. B., Zinner, E. S., and Ellis, R. R. (1999). "The Connection Between Grief and Trauma: An Overview," in Zinner and Williams (eds.). *When a Community Weeps: Case Studies in Group Survivorship.* Philadelphia and London: Brunner/Mazel, pp. 3–21.

Wilson, M. (1996). "Asking Questions," in Sapsford, R., and Jupp, V. (eds.). *Data Collection and Analysis.* London: Sage, pp. 94–120.